Soli Deo gloria.

Model Wellness

MODEL WELLNESS;
Seeking God in the 21st Century.

by

Martin Ogden

MO Books

Spencerport, New York

Images used in this book have been purchased from Deposit Photos, and are free to publish. The front cover image was acquired from Getty's Open Content Program. Biblical quotations are from the King James Version of The Bible. Personal quotations are assumed to be unique, and are attributed to the author as "MO".

Library of Congress Cataloguing in Publication Data

Model Wellness: Seeking God in the 21st Century/ Martin Ogden
ISBN 979-8-9851209-0-5 (softcover)
ISBN 979-8-9851209-1-2 (epub)
ISBN 979-8-9851209-2-9 (kindle)

© 2021 Martin Ogden, MO Books
ISBN 979-8-9851209-0-5 (softcover)
ISBN 979-8-9851209-1-2 (epub)
ISBN 979-8-9851209-2-9 (kindle)

Contents

Model Wellness

Introduction

What is spiritual wellness? Many people have sought it; most people would admit they have not experienced it.

People practice religion but still feel disconnected from God. Some work hard to seek God for long periods of time, but have not met Him. Many religious leaders are in anguish because they cannot give people spiritual life. People often cannot find a balance between reason and faith. Many people have abandoned religion and are Done with God. Their distance is real and frustrating.

This book follows one man's search to find spiritual wellness. His journey sought a find a balance between modern, rational thought, and ancient and modern religious traditions. Martin describes encounters with God that help him understand God's nature and character.

The author had an extensive journey through religion. He experienced lows and highs, and has reached a place of peace. He hopes that the reader will also find that peace.

This journey and its observations will provide guidance and help for those on their journeys.

Origins.

I was born overseas, in the middle of the 20th century, into the family of a US military officer. We lived in various foreign countries and cities in the United States and had a happy family life. My parents came from midwestern soil, and both had degrees in the sciences. They were nominal protestants, and we attended base chapels in foreign countries and attended a denominational church in the United States. I participated in some confirmation classes that did not inspire any religious sentiment, and I had no interest in religion.

I was introverted, and I was happiest reading the encyclopedia, which contained the summary of human knowledge. Reading a volume of the encyclopedia took me to foreign places, through histories, introduced me to the great thinkers and discoverers, and taught me science. One day it was Strontium, Sweden, and Switzer. Another day it would be Incans, Indium, and the Ivans. I could live the history of man, visit any area on the Earth, and see the structure and relationships of the universe. I could identify with what I read when my parents would visit the great cities, museums, and monuments of Europe. My childhood gave me a love of knowledge, discovery, and adventure.

I felt distanced, even from myself. I had little motivation to be engaged with my life or other people's lives. I had little interest in my studies in school, and attending school was a burden. My closest connection was to my brother, who was the opposite of me; he was outgoing, directed, and social. I felt that he was the other half of me, the part that I was missing.

In high school, teenagers gathered socially on Sundays, in a room at church, without supervision. One Sunday morning, an archetypical hippie visited us in the youth room and told us that we could have a relationship with God through Jesus simply by asking God. It sounded interesting, and it had no downside. I prayed, expecting nothing, and was suddenly elated. I left the room with a sense of freedom from burdens and felt connected with God. I sensed that God had given me purpose and direction for my life.

The experience changed me into a person that began to engage purposefully with life. Local teens who had similar experiences with God spontaneously started gathering, encouraged by our Jesus Freak friend and some college students involved in college campus groups. My brother had a similar encounter and was a great encourager in pursuing faith. As innocents, we rejoiced in our relationship with God and studied the Bible together, prayed, street witnessed, and fellowshipped during the last years of High School. There was a purity and zeal of belief that was exhilarating.

Our gatherings incorporated students from many religious traditions, and we had little connection with churches. There was no doctrine, creed, or trained leaders, and we read literature from campus ministries. We would have chapter-by-chapter Bible studies to encourage our faith. We read the Bible for ourselves and were encouraged to learn God's nature, listen for God's voice, and respond to Him. There was no organization, no building, no formal leaders, and there was no sense that this was permanent. After graduating from our high schools, we moved to various colleges and universities. We had reunions periodically to encourage each other and share our journeys. In time, we drifted apart, and many fell away from the faith.

I began to meet many others in different venues that were enlightened. They had peace, confidence, and a basis for existence. The expression of that enlightenment varied with each individual I met. Many had a simple, emotional faith, and others had an organized and cerebral faith. Over time I saw that the spiritual life in people could die or be corrupted.

At that time, the charismatic movement entered many religious groups. The charismatic movement encouraged ecstatic experience with God, and was viewed with suspicion by more established religious organizations. At school the Christian fellowship embodied believers across the spiritual spectrum from evangelical protestants to charismatic Catholic believers. I was immersed in a joyous, pious, interdenominational culture.

As I read the Bible, I saw statements that God acted supernaturally in believers' lives. After several years, I understood evangelical doctrine and ethics, but did not see an active God. At that point, I challenged God to "get real," or I would walk away from what seemed like a pointless experience. The following day, I was late for an early class, and I prayed that the class would be canceled. I showed up late for class and a proctor announced that the class was canceled. It was the only time professor B_____ had canceled a class in anyone's memory. Remarkable events continued for the rest of my life which solidified my faith that God was active in existence.

"Thou shalt love the Lord thy God with all thy heart, and with all thy soul, and *with all thy mind.*"   Mthw. 22:37

I came to a crossroad of reason and faith. One summer, as I traveled across Europe, I met someone who suggested visiting a nearby Christian thought and retreat center. My companion and I traveled out into the countryside and visited it. I discussed my dilemma of reconciling faith and reason with a mentor, W____. He introduced me to the "Pensées" of the pious scientist Blaise Pascal. I read the book over a few days and read that Pascal used his reason until it failed and then he used his faith. I interpreted his statement to mean that there were no limits on using reason and logic for a spiritual person. I accepted that reason does not destroy faith and that faith was for things beyond reason. Pascal's words held true for me, and I resolved to use reason and faith in full measure.

A few months later, that reckoning permitted me to have another encounter with God. I was stranded in a wino hotel in Paris. As I was praying, the heavens opened up, and I saw the immensity of the Universe and The Creator behind it. His presence flowed through me, and I was filled with His supernatural presence. The experience gave me further confidence in the existence of God. It gave me a sense that He was infinite and powerful. I understood that God was greater than anything I would experience or learn.

I graduated from college a year later, got married, and entered the working world. I worked for decades as an engineer using hard sciences and analysis. I started in manufacturing, moved to development, and then moved to research. The world I had experienced in high school and college faded away. I attended several evangelical churches with my family and then spent considerable time in charismatic churches. I held home Bible studies, lead worship, and became an elder at church.

As decades went by, I saw hypocrisy, manipulation, ambition, control, greed, lust, adultery, and divorce in the church. I did not expect such things from the enlightened. Some friends from school lost their zeal, became sidetracked, quit the faith. After several decades, I found that the teachings I had listened to seemed like formulas, programs, and morality lectures.

"Model wellness." ~MO

A lot of teaching in fundamentalist communities made me uncomfortable. As a good, spiritual person, I was expected to believe various theories that conflicted with reason and science. Simultaneously, as part of work, I travelled to multiple foreign countries with religious practices outside of Christianity, and visited their temples and shrines. These experiences created an internal conflict between reason and faith that sapped my emotional and spiritual strength. In a distressed state, I asked God to give me guidance for my dilemma. I got a statement from Him," Model Wellness." I interpreted those words as direction to seek what it means to be mentally, emotionally, and spiritually well. I resolved to journey to health.

I knew that my path would take me away from fundamentalism and move me away from historical evangelical culture. I knew that history showed that dissenters are punished, even to the point of being hung on a cross. To protect the family that I love from the jackals of society, I wrote this book under a penname.

Beginning again.

How do you begin to get spiritually well? I had heard teachings exhorting belief in things that were irrational, dysfunctional, or pure nonsense. Great faith was believing in the irrational, weak faith led to disbelief, and sin was questioning given interpretations. The people enforcing these concepts tended to be poorly educated and not astute.

In addition, I heard highly educated apologists talk about pseudo-science to justify those beliefs. The apologists comforted the uneducated masses that their flawed views were reasonable. Unquestioning belief was the only measure of faith in those environments. Outsiders were attracted by their devotion, and mistook it for faith. Some flew into the flame and were consumed like moths, while others circled warily and eventually escaped to remain sane.

"The first casualty of the religious wars is truth." - MO

People seemed to avoid truth and reason in those religious environments. That conflicted with my desire for truth and reason as a part of health. I had read that truth was esteemed in the Bible, which encouraged me to move in truth, towards wellness.

Jesus said [1]He was the way, the *truth*, and the life. In other passages, The Bible states [2]"you shall know the *truth*, and the *truth* will set you free", [3]Believers should be belted by *truth*, and [4]God's Spirit will lead us to all *truth*. Jesus stated, "Yet a time is coming and has now come when the true worshipers will worship the Father in the Spirit and in *truth*, for they are the kind of worshipers the Father seeks."[5] Yet, I saw that many religious groups were filled with untruth. People lied to themselves, lied to others, and lied to God. The laity faced two choices: play along hypocritically, or maintain association at a careful distance. My path veered away from organized religion as I sought the truth no matter what the cost.

"...who shall deliver me from the body of this death?"

~ Rom 7:24

Early in my journey, I had tasted the freedom and joy of belief, and had met others on journeys with the same experience. Later, I saw some of these people embedded in bodies of dynamic but dysfunctional believers. They accepted dysfunction without question. Others had felt the illness and rejected it, and been rejected in turn. Some were hungry for community and played the game. Some blindly followed a tradition, feeling comfortable with what was familiar. Others played along to achieve promotion and to feed their egos with organizational success. Some were playing the religious game hoping to positively impact an unwell culture. Others lived with a guilt complex, always trying to quench their guilt through self-abasement or works of atonement that proved ultimately meaningless.

---

[1] John 14:6

[2] John 8:32

[3] Ephesians 6:14

[4] John 16:13

[5] John 4:23

"Even in the village of truth, there are lies" ~MO

I spent some time with an outreach for men paroled from prisons. The program stripped away pretense and illusion to reveal the core of man. The process was done with love and in trust, leading to understanding and healing. The founder said that he wanted to see people's egos nailed to the wall when he walked into the meeting room. This program was medicine for the most desperate.

A friend, J___, had attended a meeting and, in a few hours, had been stripped down to his core. After the session, he walked away from years of alcohol abuse. He changed his life direction, and today moves along a better path. Later, my turn came, and the group stripped me of my pretensions and revealed my core. That encounter healed me of some deep anger and hurt. At the end of the session, the program leader gave me a framed poem he had been recently received for his birthday, shown below.

"i need balance between gratitude, and grievance
i need grace in that fleeting space to hear a voice whisper --
make a choice choose separation, and endless strife
or risk sharing caring love, and life
oh please oh please in my heart I care
i hope it's god alive in there
moving praying giving me a chance
to love to live to need balance" [*sic*]

After some time, I discovered that some participants were artfully lying their way through the program. I found that others used the program's tools to inflate their egos. The program founder died, and in time the program was corrupted and disbanded. I learned that even in the village of truth, there are lies. I was grateful that the program gave me the gift of valuing openness, honesty, and truth. I also learned that seeking spiritual wellness in truth was complicated. Imperfect men have a problem arriving at truth.

I had been immersed in environments that were filled with people that were spiritually and emotionally ill. I became a distanced, objective observer filled with emptiness while desperate for wellness. The experiences increased my hunger for mental, emotional, and spiritual health, regardless of cost.

21st Century science meets God.

But the wisdom that is from above is first pure,
then peaceable, gentle, and easy to be intreated,
full of mercy, and good fruits, without partiality,
and without hypocrisy. James 3:17

I had spent decades studying and applying many branches of science. The scientific culture I learned in and worked in was often antagonistic to religion. In return, the church was hostile to conventional science. Fundamentalists clung to irrational concepts that reasonable people had rejected. Scientists were taught a godless science which moved them towards atheism. Neo-atheists stated that "science killed God". Fundamentalists were becoming isolated and distanced from the common culture.

In my search for wellness, I looked at my science training. I realized that science pointed to the existence of an amazing Creator. I recall my first experience with the intersection of science and religion in the second semester of Physics at college. My Physics professor, Dr. S_____, was explaining gravitational fields on a sunny spring day. On a chalkboard, he had written the equations defining gravitational attraction between objects.

Inspired, I asked him, "Why does gravitational attraction exist"?

The Professor pointed to the equations on the board, and said: "This is how."

Again, I asked him, "Yes, but *why* is there an attraction"?

The Professor paused, blinked, thought for a second, and said, "I guess the Good Lord made it that way."

There was quiet in the room, a long pause, and then he continued with the lecture. Educators had been teaching me for fourteen years how to build a house of facts and reason. I had leaned against a wall, it had fallen, and now I looked at a larger world. I took away from the encounter that profound things lay behind the science I was learning. I wanted to see as far as possible, to move out to where faith was needed.

Several billion solar systems.

When existence is viewed through the lens of science, our World vast, and filled enormous masses and energies. Humanity immediately sees a small part of it. I learned science that presented the size and complexity of the universe as data and formulas without perspective. My conversation in the physics class hinted at the more profound mysteries that surrounded us. For example, we hear that Newton had an apple fall on his head and discovered gravity. That description trivializes Newton's discovery. The profound phenomenon he found is that all matter is attracted to all other matter, a phenomenon that we call gravity. That attraction fuels the stars when large masses of hydrogen gas coalesce into dense clouds. Gravity fuses atoms, releasing massive amounts of energy that heat the gaseous mass to create light-emitting stars. That solar energy supports life on the Earth. Planets circle the stars, kept in position by the gravitational attraction between the suns and their planets. Gravitation defines our greatest existence. Gravity is more than apples falling to the surface of the Earth; it powers the structures of the cosmos. Yet humanity does not understand the "why" of gravitational attraction.

Astronomy has slowly increased our understanding of the cosmos over the last century. Fifty years ago, man counted tens of million stars. That number grew exponentially over decades of searching. With Hubble and other powerful telescopes, we now image distant galaxy clusters having billions of stars. The number of known planetary systems now measures in the tens of billions. With that many star systems, thousands of planets have environments like Earth's. We are beginning to understand that we are not alone. That understanding is beyond what ancient men perceived of the universe.

Man lives on a thin skin of an environment on a small planet around a small sun in a small galaxy. Our existence is minuscule in comparison to the size of the universe. As I had experienced, the Creator of the universe is beyond human reason or even human imagination. In the last century, science has found that the universe we know, including physical properties such as mass, volume, time, gravity, atomic structure, and electro-magnetism, came into existence instantaneously from a point source known as The Big Bang. That Creator should be awe-inspiring and incomprehensible. I found many people perceived a small universe that could not contain an infinite God.

The Periodic Table of the Elements, which defines the universe's atomic structure, has only been understood and completed in the last few centuries. I worked with many of the 116 stable atoms in the periodic table. Their properties and applications were fascinating, and most have essential purposes. Important examples can include oxygen for animal metabolism, hydrogen to make water, iron and aluminum to create structures, copper to conduct electricity, and carbon to create a basis for life. When working with carbon compounds, you find an entrance to the vast biochemical world.

Nucleotide, phosphorus is P on the left.

Each of the hundred-plus types of atoms that exist can combine with other atoms in a few ways, but carbon uniquely creates hundreds of thousands of organic compounds. The most interesting carbon compounds are the four nucleotides of DNA. These four clusters of atoms look almost identical but define the entire biosphere, including the planet encompassing atmosphere, biomes, ecologies, and lifeforms. What is intriguing is the presence of phosphorus in every nucleotide. Without phosphorus, DNA would not exist, and without DNA, there would be no ecosphere. A planet without phosphorus would be a watery ball of mud covered with simple hydrocarbon slime. I realized that the existence of phosphor atoms is the spark of life.

DNA creates the patterns of the Plant Kingdom, from single-cell algae, to plants, to flowers, to towering Redwood trees. These various plants have many different chemical processes and structures, including photosynthesis, bark, leaves, and roots. DNA also encodes the oxygen-breathing Animal Kingdom, including worms, mollusks, insects, fish, amphibians, reptiles, birds, mammals, and man. DNA also encodes the biochemistry that defines The World's encompassing carbon cycle that exchanges carbon between the Plant and Animal Kingdoms. The DNA code for man consists of 4 billion sets of paired nucleotides, and that code is identical in every one of our 37 trillion cells. That code directs growth from a single microscopic cell that multiplies and differentiates into dozens of types of cells that form the organs of a living, thinking human being.

The thousands of DNA patterns hold the information for biochemical structures that create exoskeletons, bones, nerves, blood, flight structures, gills, light sensors, and nervous systems having encoded behaviors. The complexity of the biochemistry of life is as awe-inspiring as the astrophysics of our universe. But we are taught that this biological world evolved through an arbitrary, random processes. After understanding and working with biochemistry, I found that it irrational to assume that these phenomena are the product of randomness.

An example of the complexity and mysteries of life is the North Eastern monarch butterfly. We learn about butterflies early in our education. A butterfly starts as a tiny egg on a milkweed plant, the egg hatches and becomes a leaf-eating machine. I learned about its voracious appetite when I saw one caterpillar strip the leaves from several tomato plants in a few days. The mature caterpillar morphs into shelled dormancy and its body converts into a flying machine. Then it flies thousands of miles to a mountain range that perfectly supports its life, using new mouthparts to feed itself with nectar.

These are dry facts. I stepped back and looked at the processes in a greater context. The caterpillar has a simple brain the size of a pinhead. It never meets another caterpillar, never receives information, has no intelligence to read a map, has no GPS, and they are dispersed across a large geographical area. A butterfly emerges from its chrysalis and begins to fly thousands of miles. It flies from a large area to a single, remote valley in Mexico. It leaves the few square meters of a previous existence and flies up to a hundred kilometers each day. It does not know its destination or purpose for the journey, only that it must fly, with purpose, every day for several months.

very day, it must find nectar to fuel its journey and survive predators on land and in the air. It flies through wind and rain, over broad rivers and high mountain ranges until it arrives at its destination. The stresses of the journey are far greater than the safety it enjoyed in a few square meters of vegetation. It lives in warmth at the end of its journey as the insect life at its origins dies out in the cold. When it is safe to return, it senses that it must reverse the journey to renew life at its origin. Why does this occur? It is a deep, complex mystery that resists understanding.

Using my technical background, I considered replicating the half-gram butterfly with man-made mechanism. Optical sensors provide images to identify objects in the physical environment. Its brain is smaller than human-built microprocessors, yet contains complex code that moves it to food sources and long flights to a specific location. The airframe is amazingly light and compact. Miniscule actuators power one-cell-thick wings over thousands of miles. The actuators in the airframe are connected back to the processor through minuscule biochemical conductors. Complex algorithms in the tiny brain coordinate flight in challenging weather. In addition, the mechanism rebuilds itself several times, from egg to leaf-eating caterpillar, to a nectar-fueled flying butterfly. I had a good understanding of man's technologies: electromagnetic actuators, metals, polymers, processor chips, sensors, and navigation systems. Still, human technology does not compare to the complexity of the small butterfly. From information theory, this phenomenon defies explanation and is not a product of random chance.

Another great mystery is the regeneration of life, a process called ontogeny. A single cell with a DNA program starts to multiply. With precise timing, the cells differentiate; one cell will split into two cells, each having a different function. For instance, a cell divides, and one becomes a brain, and the other becomes a muscle. These cells multiply into 200 types of cells that form specialized organs with complex and interactive biochemical actions. The process must occur in a timed sequence to produce a viable human with trillions of cells. That process must repeat reliably for each generation of each specie for life to continue. Like an Eastern Monarch butterfly changing, the cells are directed in complex sequences. Ontology is another great mystery.

Amazing migration patterns exist for birds like the Arctic Tern, which migrates 71,000 kilometers a year between the planet's two poles. Likewise, salmon live far out in the oceans and migrate to the riverbed where they were spawned. These are complex migratory instincts as varied as the structures that define life. The organisms do not understand their migrations; they respond to various instincts. Where is the guidance information for location and timing? How do organisms know such unconscious complex patterns of life? We are taught behavioral science as facts, without context, wonder, or answering the profound "why" questions.

I saw that science and religion had split on the issue of evolution, and other scientific theories, over the last four centuries. Religion moved away from science and reason and began to exist in a bubble, decoupled from common culture. Ancient religions became restricted by incompatibility with an age of reason and facts. Religious teachers became individuals who avoided science and reason, and could only promote rigid nonsensical orthodoxy. At the same time, the complexity and vastness of scientific discoveries told us there is a Creator. Now, when I saw a human being, I understood that I was looking at something miraculous. Wellness would be holding science and religion comfortably, but I could find no peace between the them.

The great divide.

There is a divide between conservative Christians and secular society over the idea of a young Earth and an ancient Earth. Using a literal interpretation of the first chapter of Genesis, "Creationists" believe that existence was created in six twenty-four-hour time periods. They taught that the World is about 6,500 years old based on Biblical chronology. For decades, I had quietly listened to teaching by apologists for the young Earth theory. At the same time, I was learning extensively about archeology, paleontology, astronomy, geology, and biology, which taught that the Earth was billions of years old.

I bothered by unanswered questions about what I heard in church about the young Earth theory. I occasionally raised questions about the young Earth theory to some friends. Once, I asked a devout fellow technologist about the existence of light rays from stars billions of light-years away from Earth. He stated that God had made light rays in alignment and timing to create the *illusion* that creation had occurred billions of years ago. Such a Creator was a cosmic trickster, an immoral concept that sickened me.

One summer, I hiked to the bottom of the Grand Canyon, walking many miles on the hard sandstone steps. As I exited the canyon in early July after an exhausting climb, a broadcast crew from Korea met me at the top and asked what I thought of the ancient artifact. The question paralyzed me, and couldn't respond them because I was locked in theological paralysis. I told them that the Grand Canyon was marvelous. A few days later, I hiked Bryce Canyon and saw layers of sedimentary rock interspersed with layers of igneous rock. I saw that there had been multiple periods of oceanic sediment interspersed with volcanic eruptions over hundreds of millions of years in the western United States. I visited Petrified Forest and saw tropical trees in the desert that had changed into rock. I saw dinosaur tracks and bones imprints in stone at multiple sites in the American west. As I looked at these artifacts, my background told me that the process to convert organic structures into rock took hundreds of millions of years. I was sure that my friends would invoke the cosmic trickster if I discussed my observations with them.

I thought about the fundamentalist statement that the Earth's animals repopulated from a single point in the Middle East six thousand years ago. That conflicted with the information I had learned about World geography, animal groups, and animal populations. I questioned how marsupials, such as kangaroos and koalas, could have migrated over a few thousand years specifically to Australia and New Zealand. How could they migrate across deserts, mountain ranges, and vast bodies of water without leaving skeletons or signs of passing? Even more challenging was to imagine the llamas of South America, or the bison of North America, migrating from the Middle East across deserts, plains, and the Atlantic Ocean in a few thousand years. Why would penguins only migrate to the southern pole? The only answer was this: over hundreds of million years, geographical barriers to migration had evolved unique groups of animals in various areas of the planet.

When I brought up these observations, I got baffled stares and a statement of blind faith, "God made a way". Some avoided thinking about such things. That idea was an escape from reason, thought, and sanity. One simple woman of faith was uncomfortable with some observations that I had made. She looked at me and said, "you think too much." She There was no way to communicate with her, so I asked her, "What is the right amount of thought?"

As I developed technology, I found new ways of putting things together, or discovered new phenomena. Some call these concepts "inventions," which suggested they created something new. The ideas were new to man but existed before I discovered them. I realized that we don't "create" concepts; we discover what has pre-existed conceptually and then convert it into reality. The same view can be applied to creation.

Following a pre-existing design, matter and energy flowed into structures. Based on gravity, a pattern formed matter in celestial space that created stars and orbiting planets. Structures and properties pre-existed for the stellar fusion of hydrogen to create atoms that formed planets, atmospheres, and oceans. A complex plan existed for molding biochemistry and organisms into the ecosphere based on the four simple nucleotides. This evolution occurred over billions of years according to a complex design. It is analogous to pouring molten steel into a mold. The mold exists, and the fiery metal flows into the form and crystallizes. The metal assumes the shape of the pre-existing mold. The mold may not be seen, yet the object is proof that a mold exists.

I finally accepted that terrestrial life followed The Plan over billions of years. Because there are billions of planetary systems, that process will be repeated on the few planets with the prerequisite physical properties of gravity, temperature, and matter to recreate our biome. Given the billions of solar systems, we can assume that thousands of ecospheres, similar to ours, exist but are separated by millions of light-years. Recently, it has become evident there are many Earths with observations of planets around distant stars. This idea is not within the understanding of ancient men, who saw man and his environment as special. When I mentioned other inhabited worlds to the devout, they became fearful and accused me of heresy.

I needed to resolve the conflict between science and God, and reason and faith, to be well. I realized that billions of people had been confronted with the same conflict between religious practice, and knowledge and reason. The universe was bigger and older than the world understood by early man, who created ancient religions. Many modern men could not resolve the conflict and walked away from religions. Others rejected knowledge and reason to follow a mindless religion. And some practiced a cynical, cultural religion.

I was seeking wellness, and all these options were unhealthy. To be well, I rejected the craziness of organized religions and embraced truth and reason wherever it took me. I broke with the fundamentalist world, not knowing where my journey would lead. I was troubled that I would become one of those "godless liberal churchmen," an agnostic, or worse yet, an atheist.

Men's Religions.

In my youth and my career, I traveled extensively. When I traveled, I went to museums and went down into their basements, which typically held the antiquities. I saw antiquities from Babylonian, Egyptian, Greek, Roman, Amerindian, Indian, Chinese, and Japanese civilizations. All the ancient cultures had artifacts reflecting religious traditions. I saw engravings of savage gods and idols of armed demigods. A few gods were serene, or smiling. As I traveled for work, I visited Shinto, Hindu, Buddhist, Muslim, Jewish, and Christian houses of worship. Custodians explained their beliefs and customs to me, an evangelical Christian. At the same time, I was studying and teaching the Bible from Genesis to Revelation. That required me to understand and interpret the Bible from cover to cover. Over time, I saw common threads between all the religions.

The first thread was the existence of an angry or distant supreme being. The religions shared a common thread of one or more powerful beings, distant from humanity and often angry. Most Gods were like men, having human emotions and characteristics. Some of the old gods were physical embodiments of the sea, the earth, the sun, and the moon. Demi-gods personified human experiences such as love, birth, sex, war, joy, music, and pleasure. The Gods engaged in conflicts between themselves and with men. Some religions had distant, cold Gods that started the universe and observed it from a distance. These early perceptions moved forward through time and adapted to modern cultures.

A second thread was an afterlife for an eternal soul. Men have developed many stories and theories around an afterlife. Many afterlives have a judgment that directs a person's soul to a paradise or a hell, based on their actions in life. The Egyptians, Greeks, Romans, Scandinavians, and Mesoamericans had underworlds ruled by demon gods. The eastern religions did not have hells, but had cycles of reincarnation. A soul would work its way upwards or downwards through many lives, hoping to achieve enlightened perfection, Nirvana, with God. The cycle of reincarnation was working one's way out of hell into God-like perfection.

A third thread was working to appease or communicate with the Gods. These acts acknowledged a separation between God and man. They made peace with God by behaviors, activities, or material sacrifices. Egyptians, Babylonians, Jews, Greeks, Romans, Vikings, slaughtered animals, and burned goods to appease their gods. Druids, Aztecs, Babylonians, and Vikings sacrificed human beings. Self-punishment and asceticism were practiced in Judaism, Christianity, Hinduism, and Buddhism to appease and connect with the stern, righteous, and often fickle Gods. Many religions required dress, coiffure, diet, and language to appease the gods. Religions such as Judaism, Evangelical Christianity, and Buddhism needed extensive learning and meditation to understand and approach God. For them, the mind was a gateway to knowing and connecting with God.

Time, energy, pride, and resources were sacrificed to connect with God. Learning about God often involved financial payments and time commitments. These were practiced continually to maintain favor with Gods who could become distant or irritated. These believers were ever learning, ever sacrificing, and never knowing. These practices reflected and reinforced the idea that man was imperfect and separated from God.

A fourth thread was advanced practitioners dedicated to seeking and helping others connect to God. They could be called priests but were also masters, shamans, or teachers. These people, dedicated to studying their respective Deities, were a tool for the masses to maintain peace with their Gods. The laymen went about their lives and could leave the complexity of religion to specialists. These religious leaders often lived alternative existences, separated from the laity. This is true to this day, where leaders live in pampered isolation from the commoners, often in hereditary clans. They are "paid religionists", who entertain and assuage the humbled masses' religious fears.

A fifth thread was creating physical embodiments of God. Originally man carved statues or totems of these embodiments. Man's desire to personify God led to the worship of elite men, as the embodiment of Gods. Many priests became more than men, becoming demigods. Even secular leaders, Caesars, were considered gods. The desperate craving for a human embodiment of God showed man's hunger to know God concretely, or to be as God. Modern culture now reveres superheroes, celebrities, politicians, and plutocrats as minor gods.

The sixth thread was a holy structure for the presence of God. It was often presented as a center for spiritual connection with the Almighty. Be it a ziggurat, temple, cathedral, church, or ashram; man creates grandiose structures to make God's presence concrete. The degree of reverence seemed proportional to the structure's size, complexity, and amount of gold plating. Within temples around the World, rites and teaching are done at holy altars. I saw this in Shinto temples, Hindu Temples, Buddhist monasteries, and the cathedrals of Europe. Priests conduct ceremonies to gain forgiveness from angry gods. Modern religions now use simple, plain buildings for education or meditation to open the believers to small, distant Gods.

I was most interested in Protestantism. A second reformation started in Europe in the 17th and 18th centuries in response to the Age of Reason. The new sects purged some superstitions and stressed reason and perfection. It began with Lutherans in Germany and spread to Northern Europe. Reformers from England included the Puritans, George Fox's Quakers, and John Wesley's Methodists. These movements all proclaimed the need for a transforming encounter with God. Over time the various sects changed their perspective to works of perfection and intellectual codification of the spiritual. I found the remnants of the movements had devolved into an intellectual, dead orthodoxy and civic perfectionism. In those ways, they reflected the practices of the Pharisees of Christ's time. The light of their early leaders had gone out from them.

The western sects founded by the second-generation reformers lost the light, but their light grew in non-western areas. In South America, Africa, and Asia, believers arose and thrived. The enlightened on those continents are now the more significant parts of many protestant denominations. The number of the devout south of the equator now exceeds the number of the devout north of the equator.[6] Their light created rifts with the dead orthodoxies of the North. In China, indigenous Christianity has arisen in persecution.[7] Believers are sincere, knowing that a hostile society would test their faith. It was sad observing North Americans bringing their spiritual sicknesses, such as dead theology and overpowering music, to vibrant believers on those continents. The most successful natives held on to a pure spirituality and rejected western illnesses.

In the 19th and 20th centuries, Westerners started to synthesize religions with a sterile God. The new faiths often included eastern religious and scientific concepts and held God at a distance. Their goal was evolving man into godhood, or unity with a godhead, through perfection in the present life. The processes often included

---

[6] https://www.pewforum.org/2011/12/19/global-christianity-exec/
[7] *Jesus in Beijing*, David Aiken

cycles of reincarnation that were part of a spiritual evolutionary process. Themes were borrowed from eastern religious traditions, including karma and Nirvana. An example of unity with God is found in *The Phenomenon of Man* by the Jesuit Tielhard de Jardin who spent years in China. In all these systems, a process was proposed to attain the higher spiritual state as found in Eastern religions. These syncretic religions still reflected the spiritual threads of separation from the creator, and a process to appease it, with reconciliation by enlightened practitioners.

In the 19th and 20th century man created new religions based on our expanded understanding of the universe. Transcendentalism, led by the poet Ralph Waldo Emerson, emerged in elite intellectual and artistic communities. They imagined man evolving into an Oversoul. They aspired to become small, perfected demigods. In those systems, spirits lived a series of lives that eventually came to perfection in the eastern Nirvana.

The emergence of modern science and reason inspired men to create syncretic afterlives. Several modern religions, such as Mormonism in the 19t century and Scientology in the 20th century, updated reincarnation, with men ruling after death as small gods over distant, alien civilizations on other planets. Even at the end of the 20th century, some religions, created from Christianity, had leaders that were demigods. The Unification Church from Korea and the Eastern Lightning movement in China have leaders that are considered incarnate deities. Even modern physics has started to dabble in metaphysics, such as the idea of parallel universes. Instead of reincarnations over time, man's many existences are concurrent and reality depends on viewpoint.

I looked at all these religions and realized there was no evidence for an afterlife. They were imaginings of people seeking escapes from reality. They used the soul's imagination for bizarre theories. There were many common theories on the afterlife, but no credible data for the theories. It was the drive of man for superiority and perfection that drove them to these thoughts. That in itself created arrogant, escapist illnesses.

Religions use unique language to express their values and perspectives. Believers used words like enlightenment, salvation, cleared, redemption, born again, predestined, reincarnation. The language is nonsense to reason and separates believers from reason. If a practitioner tries to communicate outside the group, they are not understood because they speak an alien tongue. An outsider must enter into the culture and be immersed in the language and ethos of those religions to understand them. It seemed that all these Gods were distant and hidden in darkness and confusion, and embedded in ancient cultures. Their descriptions seemed contrary to an infinite, all-powerful God. I avoid such language in this book.

The Bible recites the history of the Jewish people's interaction with God and demonstrates the threads of religion. Abram, a simple person of faith, encounters God and walks out his faith, growing to understand himself and God in the process. Abraham's experience leads to a select people, an angry God, guilt, a temple, high priests, and sacrifices. Christianity built on Judaism and follows the common threads. Those cross-cultural threads were known by early Christian writers. They lived in societies that had many actively practiced religions. In the Book of Hebrews[8], Paul addresses the threads man's religions. He further addresses the threads in the book of Acts at [9]Mars Hill in Athens, which had an idol to the unknown god.

What is man's reaction to these religious threads? Ultimately, it proves discouraging. Religions are a treadmill of inferiority and struggle. The treadmill leaves man in a separated state with no apparent ending. Many laypeople eventually reject and despise these religions and abandon them in anger, bemusement, or denial. Many

---

[8] Hebrew 8
[9] Acts 17:23

adherents continue to practice these religions because of the threat of eternal punishment or annihilation. They hope obedience will lead to safety. Many people practice these religions to enjoy community and tradition; to prevent social shame and rejection. None of those motivations is true wellness.

I found that most Christian churches were not different from other religions. Every week, rituals occur to confess guilt and professional religionists provide moral forgiveness and social guidance. The church structures and organizations continually needed sacrifices of time, money, and piety. Christianity was filled with pagan practices such as temples, priests, holy men, demigods, altars, learning, and sacrifices. These practices were artifacts from ancient Mediterranean religions.[10] Some Christian sects had a mother and father god and minor gods, which were renamed saints. Life events required rituals to put the organization's stamp on every occasion, from birth to marriage to entombment. Many sects focused on sex and reproduction, which reflected ancient awe about reproduction, and saw women as breeding stock. The religions had been part of authoritarian rule for millennia, terrorizing the populace into compliance and enforcing social conformity.

As I learned about logic, science, and history, and applied it to The Bible, I questioned religious doctrine. If I asked questions, the teachers would tell me that these were miraculous events and that any explanation, no matter how far-fetched, could explain away any logical fallacies. Occasionally I could discuss my concerns about these things with others who were also keeping their doubts secret. We had to be quiet and not bring discord if we wanted to remain in the community. We could not discuss doubts to preserve a unity that, in reality, did not exist. My core values were truth and honesty, but religions dictated accepting nonsense to be a true believer. The Bible told me to worship God with my heart, mind, and soul [11], but the conflict between my mind and my soul distressed me. My doubt was

---

[10] Barna & Viola, *Pagan Christianity*
[11] Matthew 22:37

combined with disgust at the corrupt actions accepted by regions across the continents and ages.

Over time I found that many spiritual people were immoral and unethical. These people had partitioned morality and ethics from their religious persona. The leaders were rotten, driven by power, control, wealth, sex, and prestige. The media disclosed the continuous sexual escapades and opulence of national and local religious leaders. Believers whispered about the scandals among themselves. There was an agreement between the leaders and laypeople to ignore the scandals, and instead enjoy tradition and mysticism.

I rejected the fundamentalist community without losing a strong belief in God. It cost me relationships and separation from several communities. My belief remained strong because of the presence of God in my life. I realized I had been in an environment that lacked healthy virtues. There seemed to be no discussion of values such as honesty, truth, or reason. I valued those values, but was immersed in a culture where they were replaced by blind obedience. As I read the Bible, I saw the good that I wanted was done in men following God. However, practicing these virtues seemed to be something I could only do apart from religion.

I had seen much spiritual illness. Damaging behaviors were encouraged in the name of God, and the actions slandered Him. Many people defamed God in word and deed, leaving many hopeful people broken, or living hollow existences. The unchurched mocked religion. I had seen through some lies, and had walked away from those environments. I found myself alone for a while after leaving organized religion.

"You cannot understand light
without experiencing darkness." ~MO

After some time in the quiet, I sensed God's presence. He was light, not angry, not domineering, not manipulative. He was pure, eternal, peaceful, and wise. I felt His sorrow that men experienced such evil, but the darkness was necessary to reveal His true nature. Understanding occurred to those that sought Him sincerely. It seems that you cannot understand light without experiencing darkness. Genuinely knowing Him required abandoning the failed systems men had developed to reach God. Ultimately, God, himself had to reveal Himself to us, because humanity cannot build a system to find God.

I started re-reading The Bible with renewed purpose.

Model Wellness

In the Beginning.

I had the privilege of viewing an exhibit of the Dead Sea scrolls. In the exhibition was a small piece of papyrus, over two thousand years old, with a tiny script in Hebrew for a chapter of the book of Daniel. Next to that papyrus was the same verse from The Bible in modern Hebrew. I traced several lines of characters across each of the two pages, and each character was identical between the two passages. The scrolls are one of humanity's greatest treasures, images of the past preserved for millennia. I could see that the Bible had moved through time unchanged from the initial writing.

In my youth, I had heard textual criticism that The Bible was a fiction of man, revised many times over the centuries. Many religious scholars of the 20th century were clearly antagonistic to the Bible and its writers. Seeing the script brought forward unchanged for over two thousand years made me respectful of the honesty and integrity of the writers. Modern intellectuals had slandered the writers and scribes that had faithfully carried the text forward unchanged. But those words were interpreted in many ways.

Interpretations of the first chapters of Genesis created a division between Biblical fundamentalists and liberal theologians. Extensive arguments occurred over the nature and character of these chapters. To liberal believers, the first chapters are stories with little meaning, and stories in Genesis are taught to children more as fables rather than doctrine. To fundamentalists, they were taken as literal, word for word in the English language. I had traveled in conservative Christian circles that believed in literalism, and listened to their apologists vigorously defend the reality of the accounts. They demanded that it be interpreted in every way as "inerrant", with a subtext that the meaning of every sentence was literal. For fundamentalists, the concepts of figures of speech such as metaphor, hyperbole, allegory, anecdote, and personification, were alien and accepted only in specified contexts.

The truth is that the first chapters of the book of Genesis are a recording of oral traditions passed down over thousands of years before writing. The initial stories had been recounted over many hundreds of lifetimes before written records. The stories were common to the people groups in the Middle East. Archaeologists and anthropologists understand that truth, but literalists avoid discussing the origins of the first chapters. The written Biblical record begins later in Genesis when nomadic Jews from Egypt learned writing technology from the Egyptians. They recorded the earlier oral traditions to start a journal of Jewish history. Conservatives immediately stop the discussion of ancient oral traditions by using the word "inerrancy", which means "I can't think critically". Forbidden thinking is always a sign of unwellness.

I listened to conservatives talk about how the universe was made in six 24-hour Terran days, a snake that could talk and instantly lost its legs, fruit that imparted wisdom, a secret origin garden, an ancient boat on a mountain, how the earth was completely covered by water, and how all species of animals were on a boat for 40 days, and then repopulated the Earth. I read books by men with advanced degrees that proclaimed the truth of these phenomena. These statements caused my rational mind to reel.

With a new perspective, I realized objectively that The Bible was filled with metaphor, parables, allegories, personification, and other literary devices. I saw fundamentalists and atheists debating those literary devices, which disturbed me greatly. They both had missed the more profound truths expressed in the Bible. Rereading Genesis, I found that the stories in Genesis had a deeper meaning beyond the interpretations of liberals and conservatives. The stories of Genesis were allegories for profound truths that describe the nature of man.

Much of the knowledge we understand was not present when the stories were created. The Bible concerns the middle-east, a small part of the Earth. There was no knowledge of the continents, of the oceans, of the poles, or many other biomes. Ancient man did not know of the structure of matter, electromagnetism, astronomy, nor microbiology. Consequently, their viewpoint was very narrow and their thought and vocabulary were limited. A great example is the ancient's word "star." The Bible treats many similar lights in the sky as a "star" [12] when referring to any celestial body. Today, a bright object in the sky could be a galaxy, planet, star, or comet. We know that beyond the immediately visible lights is a vast universe with black holes, quasars, and galaxies that are invisible from Earth. That modern knowledge was not available to the writers of Genesis. However, such limitations do not negate the great truths expressed in Genesis.

The first chapter of Genesis recites the story of Creation in six days. I realized a better translation of the Hebrew word "day" in modern language would be "time period." The story then follows astro-genesis, geo-genesis, and bio-genesis. Biblical Creation starts with a Big Bang, as God releases "light". Interpreting Genesis using current science, God released highly energized protomatter into existence. That material would emit electromagnetic energy that we call visible "light." The word "spoke" in the Biblical record is a metaphor

---

[12] Matthew 2:9

for action-from-will, with meaning. There was no atmosphere at Creation that supported sound waves, and without atmosphere there can be no sound, and no speech. The word "speech" is metaphoric, something avoided by literalists.

The word "spoke" for the act of Creation has a deeper meaning. Science uses the word "bang," and The Bible uses the word "Spoke." In both cases, energy is released. From man's perspective, the term "Bang" implies an uncontrolled, violent release of energy. In the biblical perception, Creation occurs with meaning and purpose, metaphorically as "language". "Spoke" is not yelling or shouting; it is a rational, calm, and purposeful expression. The action released structures within structures within structures. The two descriptions of the event reflect two very different points of view.

Gravity compressed that protomatter to form gas clouds that compressed into stars. Genesis calls that process "separating the waters". Matter was formed in early stars, was ejected into nebulae which coalesced to form planets orbiting suns. The orbit of the Earth defined "night and day." Geo-genesis formed land, water and an atmosphere. The Bible refers to biogenesis as "the separation of the water and dry land". The Book of Genesis then recites life being forming successively in the seas, to the land, and taking to the air. I could see that the progression of the Genesis time intervals was an allegory which recited modern understanding of the universe's formation.

The six periods of Creation were recited long before any scientific understanding, and yet disclose what man has learned about the universe after thousands of years of study. The existence of a scientific recounting of the universe's origins from an early, limited perspective was God-given. The Genesis creation story demonstrated the godly inspiration of the early Bible records.

Other early religions had fantastic genesis stories that are nonsense today. I looked at Creation in different religions in ancient times. In them, anthropomorphic Gods mated or released body parts to create our World. Those creation stories can only be taken as fables in light of modern scientific understanding. Believers in such myths have a faith without reality, which requires a suspension of reason. Believers in such systems are reduced to practicing a nonsensical cultural artifact.

The third chapter of Genesis recites the creation of man. God takes clay, forms man, and gives man a spirit by breathing on him. His mate is created from one of man's ribs. Literalists focus on the sensational, the making of the women from a rib, and the hierarchical relation between Adam and Eve. That perspective misses the important concepts in the story. Key elements emerge when it is understood as an allegory.

The first is that man is made from the elements of the Earth; the writer used the word "clay" to describe man's substance. Clay, in modern terms, is a mineral composition of hydrated oxides of aluminum, silicon, and magnesium. Now, we know that our physical bodies are not "clay", but hydrocarbons, water, and some trace elements formed according to a DNA pattern. Ancient man used the closest analog to flesh, "clay" to describe our physical bodies. The key principle is that man has physical substance based on the materials of The Earth. That is our physical nature.

The second part of the story is that man has been given a Spirit, or soul, from God. God "breathes" His spirit into man. "Breathing" is a metaphor for God giving part of Himself to man, not breath from lungs. Breathing is intangible but implies an invisible substance that has energy. Man having the breath of God challenges reason, because it states that man has a supernatural spirit, given by God, and beyond the material world. That God-given spirit has the attributes of immortality, creation, vision, and mastering of nature. The story declares that there are two parts to man's existence: a physical man and a spiritual man. The narratives of the rest of the Bible describe the struggle between God, man's physical being, and man's spiritual being.

Does man have a soul? Does it make him a unique creation outside of the natural world? The concept of something more significant in man has been studied throughout history. It is often referred to as "heart", but that word comes from the ancient perception that a biological pump was the seat of the spirit. Sometimes it is referred to as "spirit", but that word also has bizarre ancient connotations. Emmerson referred to it as the over-soul. Freud referred to man's moral sense as the super-ego. Some men define it as man's reason and feeling, but those are attributes of the animal kingdom. Animals use reason to solve problems; they feel loss and joy and sacrifice themselves for others. Reason and emotion are part of the biological world, not the supernatural world.

The soul is the core of man's existence. Animals live in constrained realms with limited behaviors, and their existence is defined by foraging, eating, sleeping, and mating. Man is no different; he shares ninety-nine percent of his genome with bonobo chimpanzees. Like the bonobo, man forages, eats, sleeps, and mates. This biological life is the "clay" of our existence. But man's soul is revealed by his desire to understand the "why" of his existence, his purpose, and his origin. The urge by man's soul to meet and know The Creator manifests itself in both science and religion.

The soul's existence is shown by man's accomplishments. Man has decoded the structure of the atom, discovered and filled out the periodic table which defines matter, found the DNA code of life and now modifies it, and launched geosynchronous communication satellites that handle millions of communications simultaneously around the planet. Man has created language and writing and used them to make records of his existence, thoughts and feelings. That information is now available electronically anywhere on the Earth. Man has written music with deep philosophical themes and created art that expresses life's complexity. The other lifeforms on Earth continue to forage, eat, sleep, and mate.

Man's soul has permitted him to rise above nature and his physical limitations. Man has drawn materials from the Earth, and fashioned them into skyscrapers, dams, and continent spanning transportation networks. They dwarf anything that exists in nature. Man has created vehicles that transport people and material at speeds and distances beyond biological capability. Humanity's ships, many times in size than the largest of whales, travel the oceans. Man's planes and spaceships move supersonically, faster than the fastest animals, and into space, higher than any bird. Man has explored the plant, animal, and microbial worlds and tamed them as food, bio processors, and antibiotics. These capabilities rise above nature, make man god-like, and are products of a God-given soul.

Imagination is another God-like characteristic of man that reflects his soul. Man can conceive of what does not exist and, has created what he imagined. Man wondered about the electrical energy in lightening and harnessed it to create controlled power. He conceived of the atomic structure of matter and created materials such as plutonium, which is not found in nature. He has imagined flying like birds and now does. He has imagined visiting other planets and done so. He has imagined communication at a distance and done it. His imagination conceived of gods and created them.

Man's imagination created the early religions and stories, first orally and then as written recordings. The early tales were from a limited understanding of the physical world. Ancient mythology has now become today's fiction. Today, we describe fantasy and fictional worlds where physical limitations do not exist. These fantastic worlds reflect man's imagination.

Modern science has defined our immediate physical world and now looks at things that are beyond our reality, such as subatomic particles, astrophysics, special relativity, and quantum mechanics. As an example, in 1916 Einstein envisioned that gravity could travel in waves at the speed of light. A hundred years later, multiple LIGO observatories, a half continent apart, shone lasers through vacuum tubes 4 kilometers long. The apparatus detected infinitesimal ripples in space-time that were created 1.3 billion years ago by distant collisions of massive collapsed stars. Such science looks outside of our World with a perspective that seems mythological.

Man's imagination becomes unwell when it decouples from reality, and can lead to psychoses, paranoia and delusions. Many people operate in fantasy worlds that are distanced from reality. Their imagined worlds make them comfortable for a while, but in the long term it's destructive. In prison ministry, when people started to fantasize, we would say, "You're high; you're high, aren't you?"

Music is an expression of man's soul. It expresses our inner lives combining reason, emotion and imagination. Man's music expresses complexity far beyond anything found in nature. In most music, I could hear expressions from the soul. Music from men's souls expressed the joy of existence, victory, and frustration. I heard cries for justice, and cries for mercy. Even something simple as drum circles can subtly reflect the joy of existence and community.

Worship music could be an expression of joy in victories, love, or simply existence. Even music that denied religion and expressed nihilism, such as John Lennon's *Imagine* or Joan Osborne singing *(What if God was) One of Us,* implied morality beyond nature. The singers deny a creator, but express ideas beyond nature using musical technology far from the natural world. The difference between their music and their existence is ironic. Even musicians of dark music, such as grunge, cry about injustice, citing unseen moral laws. They cry for justice, but do not know the author. Music, along with speech and thought, points to man's soul, something greater than nature.

Documentaries compare phenomena in other creatures to man's achievements. The comparisons fall woefully short. An ape using a stick to extract termites or an otter using a rock to break open clams, or a termite mound do not compare to man's great works, such as orbiting communication satellite, or Handel's *Messiah.* Scientists compare the meaningless twitter of birds, or grunts of whales to man's symphonies, which have many different voices and reflect a cosmic perspective. These modern comparisons are sad reflections of people sensing spiritual things without context.

When a man accepts that equality, he denies his marvelous soul and denies its Donor. I concluded that man has a supernatural soul. Man's creations reflect a soul seeking to know its creator. The soul is spiritual "phosphorus" that energizes man to move beyond his physical limitations. Based on the great works of man, how can anyone not believe that man has a spirit expressing itself, and that it is beyond nature?

The Garden of Eden story is sensational, with a secret garden, naked people, snakes with legs that talk, forbidden fruit, magical trees, and angelic beings with flaming swords. My mind spun during explanations of the truth of talking snakes and magic apples. These elements were taught vigorously in ways that missed profound truth. It's an allegory, and when sensationalism is removed, a key observation remains.

The story states that man, by his own choice, chooses to be an independent moral agent. That action results in a willful separation from God. This story is the basis of the Judeo-Christian tradition. That perspective assumes that man has a soul, and that soul chooses to be its own moral law. The story ends with humanity's abandoned, separated from God. Most people would agree with the story's conclusion that they are separated from God. Subsequent tales in Genesis demonstrate the consequences of owning moral authority. It ends in damaging actions, and man begins to reconnect with God. That search leads to shame, priests, temples, and sacrifices.

The story of Noah is another early story in Genesis. I listened to men trying to apply scientific explanations to validate the account. Listening to those explanations created stress between my reason and my faith. Apologists created elaborate explanations of how water could cover the entire surface of the Earth, and how the animals that rebuilt life were stored and fed for 40 days. They described how the Earth was repopulated by from a single place in the Middle East six thousand years ago.

After rejecting the idea of an Earth covering flood, I considered that it could have some validity. The Earth could never be completely covered with water, but an early civilization, "The Known World" to the writer, could have existed in a basin that was flooded cataclysmically. Looking at the map of the Middle East, it's conceivable that such a civilization inhabited one of four basins: the Persian Gulf, the Red Sea, the Mediterranean Sea, and the Black Sea. These basins all have narrow straits to large bodies of water. The straits could have been blocked, leaving the basin dry. They could have been breached, and the seas flooded the basin and destroyed the inhabiting civilization. After being inspired by God, a righteous man could have built a refuge for his family and livestock to rebuild civilization. The mechanics are not important; the fundamental principle is that when humanity is refined to a few noble individuals at the end of the story, they devolve back into immorality.

Genesis starts with a few prehistoric stories but soon becomes historical and literary. Biblical history tells of a how a man, Abram, and then a people, struggle to understand and respond to God. Man's understanding of God increases over generations of interactions. A critical event was Moses going up to meet God on Mount Sinai. Moses asks God for His name, and God says his name is YHWH, "I AM".[13] It's an incredible statement because it embodies the infinite; there are no limitations in that expression. Other religions in that era had Gods based on man, animals, and astronomical bodies. They were finite compared to the Infinite. Other gods were based man's immediate existence; "I AM" reflected an infinity that separates the Biblical God from other ancient gods. Like the six days of Creation, that perspective was received from Him, and was not created by man.

As I reread The Bible, I concluded that it is an imperfect, but honest, accounting of people's interactions with God. It reflects the writers' cultures and ethos, and incorporates significant allegories. The writing provides profound insights into the nature of man and God. The history and literature are told objectively, with flawed characters and societies. Men murder, rape, steal and lie. The societies are filled with polygamy, misogyny, slavery, tribalism, incest, castes, genocide, and cruel totalitarian states. The Bible does not endorse these, but is an honest recounting of a history. The many failures in the Bible reflect the honesty of the recording.

In The Bible, people as a group fail, leaders fail, ordinary people are called to greatness. It is a history of people seeking God as they live in challenging situations. The colorful details of those stories and mores of ancient societies are often not pertinent to today's culture. The Bible does not speak to many of the ethical dilemmas of the current age. I read the stories in the context of men seeking and encountering God, and walking out faith in Him in imperfect circumstances. Most people in The Bible fail at this. What is helpful to a reader is seeing people encounter God, come to understand Him,

---

[13] Exodus 3:14

be inspired, and work good in broken people and societies. That work of the reborn is true today, as it was in ancient cultures.

I re-read the New Testament, reading the text objectively and critically. I did not see an organized, comprehensive set of writings as we see in modern literature. It is a series of short stories from secondary sources, recorded decades after the events. The gospels of Mark and Luke were written by people that were not immediate associates of Jesus. None of the gospel writers were old enough to have been present at the origins of Jesus. Many events are of solitary individuals or encounters by a few people. Mark is an early outline for Mathew and Luke, both of whom added further detail. John is a unique narrative, sourced outside of the first three gospels. It's apparent that the authors used multiple sources for stories passed down over many decades. This understanding led me away from the fundamentalists' perspective that they were "perfect" or "complete".

I found that there were inconstancies. For instance, Luke talks of an immediate return home after Jesus' birth, while Mathew relates a time in Egypt. In the feeding of multitudes, there is a difference in number. In Mark, Christ is taken immediately to Golgotha, but He is sent to The Sanhedrin in Luke. The four gospels differ on Christ's last words. Teachers would carefully avoid the drinking of poison and handling snakes in Mark 16. They avoid John 14:13, which says that we can ask anything in Jesus' name and it will be done. There are two different genealogies of Jesus in the Gospels. The listing of the tribes of Israel in Revelations was inconsistent with the Old Testament. Most of the writers were not expert writers, creating short, simple stories.

The text reflects a life with God, and is not written word-by-word by God in a perfect way. Within the books, there are different perspectives on spiritual life. Matthew's sermon on the mount portrays a life of simple freedom. John's Last Supper describes a supernatural life. Paul, in Romans, lays out a logical theology. These men knew the same God, but had different perspectives. These passages cannot be really understood or taught without having the spiritual life that underlies them. Despite the variation and uncertainties, the spiritual life behind the text is powerful and life-giving. It was written by honest men, who delivered great truths in an imperfect world.

I listened to teachers' attempts to explain away discrepancies, but their reasoning was faulty. They justified their explanations by the principle of "presuppositional truth". It meant that the Bible was perfect and exact, and believers were free create absurd explanations. That perspective ignored objectivity, reason, and truth. That disconnect led believers to avoid reason and truth. When they hid form objectivity, they revealed their understanding that the text was imperfect. I found that The Bible survived quite well when viewed objectively.

The letters after the gospels reflect Christian history and practice after the death of Jesus. They reflect conflict and disagreements from the very beginning of The Church. The letters from Paul, reflecting his reason, appealed to people craving a structure that reduced spirituality to formulas. I met many believers fixated on Paul's writings, which provided them with a logical, reasoned view of Christianity. Books written by John fed the mystics. Both John and James fed the people craving guilt and order. The books reflected different spiritual perspectives of one faith. My personal studies had started in the logical Pauline epistles, then moved to an intense study of the Old Testament. I returned to the source of my rebirth, the words of Jesus in the Gospels.

Along with other apocalyptic passages, the Revelation of John describes the World's end in a supernatural cataclysm. The text has been a source of hysteria over the last two thousand years. In the late 19th century, John Darby modernized the Apocalypse, and his view now permeates the modern church. The goal of apocalyptic teaching seemed to be to scare people into finding and clinging to God. The text inspired fear for millennia, a fear that has been brought forward into the 21st century. I emerged from a culture, which was filled with terror about impending doom. I realized that it was mentally, emotionally, and spiritually unwell.

As I reread the apocalyptic verses, I understood what had been avoided by modern fundamentalists: the prediction, by Jesus, that the Apocalypse would occur within His generation[14]. The revelation of John is a cryptic description of the destruction of the Jewish Temple and homeland in 70 AD. I saw hidden references to Rome, the mad Emperor, and the Jewish Temple, and the destruction of Judea. The Revelation of John revealed the truth of Jesus' prediction about the devastation that was to come. The text is relevant only to that geographical area and era. We live in a larger world, several millennia removed from the writings. Knowing that the Apocalypse had already occurred brought me to peace.

I concluded that The Bible is history and observations, dye on papyrus, ink on vellum, ink on paper, and most recently, data bytes. The words describe individuals' actions, thoughts, feelings, and interpretations about encounters with God over thousands of years. The words are not written by cynical manipulators that creatively wrote fables. The words are intense, sincere descriptions of interactions with God. The records are not comprehensive and reflect the imperfections of the writers and cultures. Paul, one of the writers, describes our spiritual understanding as "seeing through a mirror, dimly"[15].

Reading The Bible provides a measure of understanding, but they are the writer's experience in certain times and contexts. Often, words are not pertinent to a reader's situation. The enlightened can learn about the nature of God and apply what they read to their life; however, the text itself does not give spiritual life[16]. I had met many people that had read the Bible, but without spiritual enlightenment. People understand spiritual truth by encountering God and walking with him over time. Spiritual life is not acquired through knowledge and study of ancient texts.

---

[14] Matthew 24:34

[15] 1 Corinthians 13:12

[16] 2Corinthians 3:6

What happens when you stop believing that the stories are not literal but strong metaphors, that the church is dysfunctional, and that spiritual illness is paralysis? What happens when there is confusion about what is truth and fable? My choice was to move to health by using truth, reason and objectivity. That led to distance from the communities of my origins. It required work to find understanding and finally, to find peace.

The supernatural

My journey started in fundamentalist Christianity. I had challenged God early in my spiritual life to be active, and He was. Fundamentalists wanted to take every word in The Bible literally, but their religion fell apart at the supernatural. I had listened to many rationalists explain away the supernatural in the Bible. They shied away from the idea of supernatural acts in the present. It seemed that if The Bible had validity, the supernatural acts in The Bible would continue to occur. Believing that, I expected to see supernatural actions in my life.

I had supernatural experiences early in my journey, and sought out churches that accepted an active presence of God. I had many improbable events occur in my life, actions that went far beyond everyday experience. I experienced supernatural wonder multiple times. I met others with similar experiences, and many of us gathered in Pentecostal churches, which accepted the supernatural action of God today.

Pentecostalism holds the powerful premise that God is supernaturally active in the world. As I continued my journey and discarded unwell things, I questioned the nature of my Pentecostal experiences. I had multiple questions about them. Were they real or psychological? Were the actions inspired by God or just random occurrence? I had my faith based on reason, but experiencing the supernatural was another pillar in my relationship with God.

Many Pentecostals spoke of continuous supernatural actions by God in their lives. Many of them gave spiritual significance to every action, every unexpected or trivial event. Others believed that they could command God to act, using faith, speech, or actions. As I lived in these communities, I was able to see the results of such behavior. Frankly, I saw no truth in many stories about the supernatural. In addition, they were living in stress due to denying reality. Many people were left wondering what happened, why it didn't work. They questioned the experiences, or moving to churches that denied the supernatural. Despite evidence to the contrary, many faithful showed their zeal by disconnecting from reality and committed to a Pentecostal fantasy life.

I was disturbed by the sickness in Pentecostalism. Some told me they were walking in health because of their faith, while quietly taking medications and having medical procedures. Their health failed, as they nobly declared that the illnesses did not exist. They were trying to honor God by losing their sanity. They tried to persuade other people to join in their delusions.

Some engaged in mind science, imagining a commanded reality. They feared that disbelief expressed in thought, speech, or action broke the spell. Some experienced tragedy and continued to believe that imagining, speaking, or seeing an alternative outcome would change reality. People around them remained silent, fearing that truth would destroy what was perceived as faith. Their behavior and statements were psychotic, narcissistic, and megalomaniacal. Repression and denial are wonderful tools that God has given us for dealing with suffering, but they are not healthy in the long run. I chose truth and heath and moved away from Pentecostalism.

An essential question for me became: does God enter our reality and act in our lives? There were many supernatural stories in religious writings and in people's personal stories. Most historic supernatural tales were outrageous and ugly, and I questioned the reality of those experiences. However, I had personally experienced some highly improbable events, and been part of other's improbable events. The most unlikely event I experienced was when I decided to take a term abroad in college. I prayed, asked for a description of my host family, and wrote it down. One hundred and twenty families offered to host thirty American students. My family was picked for me according to my description. When I arrived, my family told me that their daughter had been sick unto death, and they had prayed that if God healed her, they would host an American student who would show them the way to God. The daughter was healed, and they requested to be a host family for an American student. I arrived, introduced them to God, and they have been serving Him ever since.

In another case, a member of my Bible study group had prayed for and received the name of her future husband. She mentioned the name to me. I was skeptical because I had never met anyone with that last name. Three months later, she met the man for the first time, married him, and they have had a successful marriage for many decades. I had prayed for people who were not of right mind on two occasions, and they became sane instantly. Once was in a decrepit trailer at a migrant camp, and once at noon on a busy city sidewalk. One of our children started to suffer from nightmares, and we found and removed a fetish doll that had been under their bed. Their nightmares stopped. We never told the child about our actions.

In another instance, I had been led to talk to a man about a critical truth, and had driven to his workplace. He looked at me in amazement, and asked why I was there because it was his day off. He had stopped by work for a few minutes to check on the business, and I had appeared with a timely message. I delivered the message he needed to hear and returned to my work. In another case, a desperate woman asked elders to pray for her daughter, who had been diagnosed with leukemia. The elders did not believe in spiritual healing, but did as they were asked. The woman's daughter was cured without medical intervention, and lives healthy today.

I was amazed that these things had happened. These, and other events, provided evidence of a spiritual realm interacting with reality. The probabilities around such events led me to conclude that God interacts with His Creation. I noticed in these experiences that people had little agenda, and the events occurred as people were directed by God[17]. As my mentor, M____, told me once, "Pray it easy."

This pattern also appeared to be the case for the supernatural in The Bible. People connected with God and acted upon that guidance. The actions of God were different from the miracle workers in the circuses, who promised man-directed power and control. Those power ministries come from man's need to master his environment by taming fire, domesticating animals, and taming the Almighty. The truth is that Man does not control the Almighty. The Almighty moves quietly, usually unseen by man, and God's actions are often a surprise to men.

God's actions in the universe are separate from the intents of man, and move in directions not easily seen by men[18]. If a person aligns themself with God's intentions, they can see the actions of God. God's actions are a spiritual river, with power and direction. If a man sets himself in a stagnant or dry area, there is no motion, no spiritual life. As he aligns with God, activity begins, and there is spiritual life with observable actions of God. In the same way that the physical world formed with intent, man's life is empowered when he is responsive to God.

---

[17] John 5:19

[18] Isaiah 55: 8-9

I found many people were stubbornly set, demanding that God behave or act in a given way. Those believers are spiritually inert and powerless, stranded by their arrogance. Some tried to command the waters of God to flow to them. They stood in stagnant ponds and dry stream beds, wondering why they can't see god's actions. I accepted the supernatural as part of wellness and truth despite the dysfunction of many believers.

Jesus

I looked back at my spiritual origin, which started with Jesus. I saw that the Jesus of the gospels disrupted the religious orthodoxy. He did not write texts, create institutions, or organize doctrinal statements. His life and teaching were recorded as short stories and parables. He taught and reached common people for the most part outside of religious institutions.

Jesus appeared in a culture that had interacted with God for over a thousand years. His origins and environment were defined by Jewish history and religion. Jesus was immersed in a society defined by the religious threads of man's religions: a disgruntled God, guilt, a spiritual elite, a temple, and sacrifices. Jewish culture was little different from other religions in the area, other than being monotheistic. I had heard criticism of the ancient Jewish culture and agreed that the critics were right. Ancient Judaism was tribal, had plural marriages, slavery, social stratification, and treated women as property. In particular, the periodic spiritual uncleanliness[19] of women disturbed me, a husband and father of daughters.

The cultural disconnects became apparent to me as I taught Sunday school to 8th graders. I was teaching the key elements of The Bible to 8th graders over a year, starting from Genesis. After a few months, a bright child asked me, "Why were there plural marriages and so much fighting in the Old Testament"? I was stunned by the question. I was inspired to state that those people lived in an imperfect world obsoleted by the arrival of Jesus, who taught us a better way. That encounter is burned in my memory. That bright girl eventually walked away from faith. My brief statement could not overcome the impact of growing up in a dysfunctional culture.

So, who was "Jesus"? Jesus claimed to be God incarnate, something that discomforts many modern religionists. I had come to believe He was God because I had been transformed and experienced His presence for decades. As I looked at Him objectively, I saw that He rose above society and organized religions. His "good news" was that He would connect God with man directly. He obsoleted man's structures to meet God. He stated that God loved man as a Father and Creator, and wanted a direct relationship between man and God.

Jesus broke all the threads of man's religions. God was not angry and distant; He was a kind, a good Father that loved men. Men were not servants of God; they were beloved children. God's presence was not in a building but present within people's being[20]. Men did not need intermediaries because God Himself would speak to man directly. Finally, He demonstrated God's love for mankind as a martyr, forgiving them as He died an unjust death.

---

[19] Leviticus 15:9

[20] Jeremiah 31:33-34

Jesus did not offer a peaceful life. He spoke the truth directly to men. The Prince of Peace and Love Personified promised conflict within families, and with societies, and with religious traditionalists. He warned that societies would be hostile to His followers. He was killed for upsetting the religious authorities and by the fear of an administrator. Pilate famously said, "What is truth" when confronted by Jesus. Any modern intellectual would make the same statement. Afterwards he declared himself innocent of murder, and agreed to the killing of Jesus. Jesus' last words were, "Father, forgive them for they know not what they do." His resurrection changed his disciples into a movement that covered the Earth with billions of followers in every culture and every social class over two thousand years.

Jesus taught that man connected with God by trusting that God himself had offered a connection to man. When people encountered Jesus, He created that connection. As He met people, their being was laid bare, and they were healed and enlightened. Their life directions were changed. These encounters occurred within His own culture, and the adjacent Roman and Samaritan cultures.

A great thinker or theologian could have proposed His message, but there would have been no spiritual power in it, no proof of that it was true Why Jesus? God wanted people of any estate to easily and freely connect with Him. God chose a common man as His vehicle. Jesus was not a scholar, a king, or general. He entered existence after the establishment and documentation of religious practices that revealed man's religious yearnings and constructs. He did it at the intersection of the three major continents to reach out to all people. By physical manifestation, God entered reality to interact with people, to define and heal men's souls and bodies. He demonstrated authority over creation by editing people's lives. Finally, He resolved the separation between man and God in His death. In all these contexts, Jesus' existence makes sense. Connecting with God was beyond a man's capability, but God made a way.

The most notable example of connecting with God was Jesus' encounter with Nicodemus[21]. Nicodemus was a good and learned man. When he looked at Jesus, Nicodemus saw something beyond goodness and wisdom. He saw an active spiritual life in Jesus. Jesus' truths and spiritual power revealed Nicodemus' spiritual emptiness as pious follower of religious tradition. When Nicodemus asked Jesus how to connect with God, Jesus told him that he had to be born again, to become spiritually alive.

Fundamentalists turn the words "born again" into a process, such as praying, and baptisms. I saw many go through these actions without evidence of spiritual life. Some people reacted emotionally, or enjoyed the zeal of a new and healthier religious norm, for a while. But life is a gauntlet that reveals truth over time. It is a gauntlet that beats the lies out of people. Despite an intense initial zeal, I often saw no long-term spiritual life in many lives. After a time, their lives gave lie to the declaration that they had connected with God. These false believers never truly met God. I *did* see many that had their lives redirected and empowered over time; I was one of them. Those that had experienced God had perspectives and actions that held up under stress. Being born again was connecting with God, and interacting with Him throughout life.[22] It was not through a formula.

When you read the biographies of historical figures, you see men enlightened with spiritual life. The life of Martin Luther is a good example. For years, he desperately sought God as a self-denying monk and religious scholar at the University of Wittenberg. His mentor suggested that he teach a class on the book of Romans. Luther found spiritual life when he grasped that relationship with God was created simply by accepting God's healing. He connected to God in simple faith, not because of his decades of intense religious practice and academic study. In 1518, Luther wrote of his experience

---

[21] John 3

[22] Matthew 7: 15-23

"Here I felt that I was altogether born again, and had entered Paradise itself." His life took a powerful new direction, and he brought light to hundreds of millions over many ensuing centuries.

John Wesley was another pious man who had dedicated himself to working for God. He failed as a missionary and was returning from America on a ship. The ship was on the verge of going under, and he was terrified. He saw Anabaptist families calmly preparing to meet God. He became aware of his spiritual bankruptcy. He was enlightened after attending Anabaptist prayer meetings in London for several days. He wrote in 1738," I felt my heart strangely warmed.". His life became empowered, and he gave spiritual life to millions.

Blaise Pascal was a nominal believer but experienced God in a form that he described as "Fire", in 1646. He documented the encounter, keeping a record of the event on his person at all times to remind himself of what he had experienced. That encounter carried him into powerful scientific discoveries while writing about his living perspective on God. A book he wrote, *Pensees,* is a powerful defense of Christianity, and considered a masterpiece of the French Golden Age of Enlightenment.

In fundamentalism, spiritual rebirth was framed as a legal contract with God. But as I read about people encountering God, there was no complexity, no dogma, no contract. People met God in moments and came spiritually alive. The encounters changed their life direction, as a connection with God guided them with purpose. That change was profound and enduring.

The most remarkable example of that connection is the [23]thief on the cross, who asked to be remembered in Paradise. Jesus told the thief that the thief would be with Him in Paradise that day. That perfect example shows the simplicity of connecting to God by

---

[23] Luke 23:43

trust. There were no good deeds, no pious actions, no religious obligations, no doctrines to learn. True faith and God's response are simple and instantaneous. This brought up the question,

"Why has man made faith so complicated?" ~MO.

Following

What is faith? I had observed mankind's religious experiences, which could be intellectual, emotional, or experiential. Men spent thousands of hours debating the nature of God, and building philosophical constructs to explain His character, nature, and operation. When I considered the immensity of The Creator and the complexity of life, thinking our way to God seemed futile [24].

In the charismatic movement, I experienced great emotional outpourings. I participated in and led moving musical worship. I saw worship leaders working hard to bring God's presence into gatherings. I concluded that these events were summoning of a distant God, and did not reflect an all-present, all-powerful God. I found that participants often had intense experiences with little impact on

---

[24] 1 Corinthians 3:19

their lives[25]. The audience was there to temporarily experience strong religious feelings. It was a manufactured emotional experience, often with little spiritual substance. There were calls to "bring God's presence", but I wondered why an Almighty God would *not* be present everywhere at all times. Indeed, there was often a pride that focused on creating a moving experience. Worship music became performance music, not a led collective response. Performance music increased in complexity to permit corporate worship. The laity became people who sought an emotional high for the next week. I could see musicians and singers lost in the music itself, not projecting any spiritual life. Those experiences ultimately proved to be shallow and faded over time. I walked away from self-absorbed worship experiences.

My faith sensitized me to suffering in others. I counseled, supported, and encouraged many in the faith. I helped people in need during their times of weakness and failure. I shared faith with others, and saw their lives come alive as they followed God. Service to others seemed to flow naturally from a relationship with God. I also met people who sacrificed their lives in service to humanity without spiritual content. They were often motivated by guilt and a need for meaning. I saw that service can be a *response* to God's presence, but was not in itself a way to move with God.

I found that faith grew by letting God's presence guide and empower me. As I interacted with God over time, I learned more about Him than any lecture, emotional experience or works could reveal.[26] God says His name is "I AM" and so "we are". Our existence in, and motion through life, reveals God's presence in our lives. This is more "eastern" in understanding than the western thought that frames faith through reason, and piety. We grow in spiritual

---

[25] Matthew 15:18

[26] 1 Corinthians 13:1-3

understanding by letting God guide our lives. Following God makes life easy, and our struggles easy.[27]

It is difficult living simply by faith, believing in a benevolent God. What we see and experience reveals failures, pain, and injustices. In those situations, we ask ourselves, "Is this a creation of a loving God? Do we have a relationship with Him?". Healthy faith is walking in trust that God is with us and working through us, even when our minds, emotion, and experience disagree. We have faith, but we do not reason or feel with it; we act on it. When God's presence supernaturally empowers our lives, faith is revealed.

We contain a reflection of God; consequently, we have a sense of good and evil. When we err against our internal moral law, we feel guilt and shame. In our guilt, we want to undo the action, fix the hurt, and repair the damage we have done. It is easy to scold ourselves, sacrifice our pride, or engage in religious activities to assuage our guilt. It is harder to believe that the Creator still loves and accepts us when we fail. I saw many enlightened turn back to a religious life of guilt, shame, and works that was spiritual death. They did not have enough trust in a gracious, gentle, and forgiving Father. They preferred the comfort of rituals that did not require faith.

The Bible describes God's presence as a coach and guide[28]. Unfortunately, many of the people I encountered were driven by torment and fear, and mistook them for God's leading. Teachers would encourage spiritual guilt to drive believers to "correct" behavior. This wrote fear on people's faces, into their speech and actions. I encouraged the guilt-ridden to look at what was driving them. I urged them to receive God's kindness and release their guilt. Often, the concept of spiritual freedom was too frightening to many, and they needed to huddle in their dungeons of guilt.

---

[27] Matthew 11:28-30

[28] John 16:5

"Great truth is very expensive." ~MO

The most significant growth in my faith occurred in crises. I wasn't aware of it during those times.. In dark tunnels, God's presence carried me through. It was less action and more "being". Later in my life, my brother went through a series of tragedies, each uglier than the previous one. The mechanics of the descent were shocking and could not be understood. I was left numb as his slow destruction unfolded. I prayed for and saw his miraculous recovery from death, but he ended up physically, emotionally, and spiritually crippled. When he finally died, all I felt was relief that it had ended.

I also felt that half of me had died. For me, emotionally, my brother's descent was ugly and unreasonable. I had every right to be angry and bitter. I lost mental, physical, and experiential trust in God, and walked around as an empty shell. I sat numbly through sermons, but theology could not heal my brokenness. Worship did not lead me to peace. I went to Christian counseling. The counselor wanted me to make a leap of faith that God had redeemed my brother's life in his last moments. I knew that this was not the case, and all these "solutions" to grief were ineffective.

On a warm spring day, ten years after his death, I visited his gravesite. After a few minutes, I sensed peace for him and me. After a long season of grieving, I realized that I was experiencing God's healing. It wasn't based on understanding, it was not accompanied by joy, and it was not a dramatic experience.[29] This was a faith revealed when every crutch was taken away. I had been "based", reduced to raw faith without physical trappings. Through that experience, I learned that faith is not thought, not reason, and not pleasant experiences. It's something profound and intangible that comes from God, and grows and is revealed by the fires of life.

---

[29] Hebrews 11:1

The people in the Bible that experienced God found Him far away from civilization. Biblical examples include Abraham wandering in foreign lands, Moses being banished to the Sinai desert, David as a rebel in the wilderness, Jesus in the Judean wilderness, and Paul's time in the Arabian desert. As they moved away from the noise of civilization, they came to know and experience a God greater than their existence. This understanding is the opposite of the traditional path of listening to teachers, and practicing religious rituals in buildings filled with holy men and guilt. It is grasped in the quiet of barren spaces. After these men came out of their deserts, mankind's religions were weak and powerless compared to meeting the living God. I had gone through a wilderness in my brother's suffering, and I would never return to the illnesses of mankind's religions.

Religions require learning a context and doctrine. Often in the process, the brain and reason become the tools to build a spiritual life. Dinesh D'Souza observed that spirituality is not based on knowledge, or PhDs would be closest to God.[30] Many religions use education to create spiritual guides, assuming that information and reason build faith. Many of the churches I attended centered spiritual growth on learning the Bible. Many other religions also create institutions filled with people learning their way to God. Unfortunately, that process denies the existence and operation of the supernatural, in favor of man's reason. There was an intellectual pride that substituted for spiritual depth. Those practitioners lacked empathy and care in a cold, brutal existence.

Those religionists are expert practitioners of the arts of reason and persuasion. They are the descendants of the Age of Reason, when science began to understand the World in precise, objective language. That Age was based on societies returning to Greco-Roman logic and philosophy. Believers adopted that reason and logic and reduced religion to analytical constructs, theories, and creeds. The new direction paralleled the rise of science in the secular world.[31]

---

[30] D'Souza, *What's so Great about Christianity,*

[31] Viola and Barna, *Pagan Christianity*

There is comfort in having a comprehensive, logical explanation of the World. However, the systems fall apart when one includes God's supernatural nature. Logical preachers would encourage people to ignore experience, and perceive only a structured world. Those worlds were spiritual prisons for very small lives. They can quote the Great Commission in Matthew 28, which is very objective, but not Mark 16, which incorporates supernatural manifestations. The systems fall apart in the face of life's unpredictability and the supernatural. The supernatural makes rationalists feel uncomfortable, which is fended off by reasoning away spiritual manifestations. Because I had experienced the supernatural and found it valid, I found their reasoning was flawed.

Rationalists focus on the teachings of Paul. Paul was formerly Saul, a member of a strict and ordered Jewish sect that excelled in discipline, structure, and definition. Paul's writings reflect his origins, are filled with logical explanations and structures. They were based on his training in Greco-Roman logic and reason. His teachings form the basis of the fundamentalist church and compatibility with modern rationalism. That focus reflects fear of the irrational, supernatural portions of scripture. Biblical literalists have a restrained perspective on the greatness of the Almighty. They and their god reside in a neat, orderly box. That God is not the Almighty.

I once told an acquaintance that I was a believer after working with them for a while. When I revealed my faith, he said," Oh, you are not like the others". Instantly I knew what he meant. He had encountered rationalizing believers that were hard and judgmental. He sensed that people that knew God should be filled with gentleness, warmth, and joy. He concluded that the hard, joyless believers he had met were not really Christians. His observation left me empty, knowing that he had revealed a fatal flaw in the fundamentalist belief system. I had several other encounters with individuals who made similar comments.

Some churches concentrated on the psyche and civics. Platitudes and psychological principles focused on self-acceptance that would create successful marriages, parenthoods, and work. The teaching was little different than the secular motivational teachers that taught mind science. Both secular and religious programs promoted self-belief that would lead to success and happiness. The teaching struck me as neurotically self-absorbed, with a selfish perfectionism that had no spiritual basis.

Man's different religions and denominations had incorporated mind-science into their belief systems. I met many poor wretches that had been trapped in it. They tried to use denial, repression, and fantasy to cope with reality. The prison program I had attended looked at such people and would say, "You're high; you're high, aren't you?". I was startled and confused by their meaningless psycho-babble, which had no rational content. They talked about complex theories with no rational basis. It was frightening how they would accept their teachers' nonsense. Ultimately, they were escaping reality and truth, and they were unwell.

There were cheerleaders for God. They were well-meaning, enthusiastic people that wanted to inspire others through zeal, music, and passion. I confess I was involved in the worship movement for a time. The exhilaration of those environments inspired people to mania. As I lived in that culture, I was able to see the backside of the tapestry. People that turn on by pressing the happiness button in worship had little depth. Happiness alone fails under the stresses of life. They were pressing the happy dopamine button like a lab rat to escape reality. They often wandered into lies and evil by their suppressed lusts. I got off that drug.

There was no shortage of guilt mongers across the spiritual spectrum. The older religions had a spiritual elite that ruled through guilt. The Gods were angry or disappointed with men, and men had to grovel and ask forgiveness to please them. The primary instrument to control the faithful was the terror of pain in the afterlife.

Grovellers would receive weekly doses of forgiveness from the religious elite over lifetimes of sacrifice. Life in such a system becomes a passage through guilt, shame, and fear. Ceremonies were conducted continuously to confess guilt, repent, and receive atonement. The grovellers had impressive piety and humility in that darkness. I met many who had fled the environment and were filled with hatred towards a judgmental God and organized religions.

Spiritual guilt is based on ancient, dark instincts that provide structure and order. Such things are comfortable and known to the masses, and require little thought, only obedience. I observed many people raised in freedom return to those traditions to find an ordered foundation. I also saw many that realized that the order and structure are based on archaic systems with little relevance to life. They become tired of guilt and a life of cowering in fear. Many left the comfort of structured religion and found themselves empty or living for pleasure. They had missed a different path that led to freedom from guilt and shame. Instead, they chose to live in anger or selfishness.

I spent time in organizations run by entertainers; strong, charismatic leaders who created marvelous spectacles. People would be dazzled with emotional appeals and psychological tricks. The Forer effect is used in introductory psychology classes to demonstrate the basic gullibility of man. A test is given to detect the test-taker's personality. A random description that speaks favorably is provided as feedback. Test subjects report that the random description was typically 86 percent accurate. The religious showmen used that gullibility to dazzle the masses. People were desperate to believe in these god-like men, and followed them to be delivered from despair. Many were satisfied with cheap miracles and empty promises. Most were left living with empty, broken lies in the long run. They never got to wellness.

Jesus challenged entrenched religious authority by stating that the religious structures were not needed, and even a hindrance to meeting with God. His converts were instantaneous, without the complexity of ceremony, doctrine, or study. The organized religious groups at that time opposed Jesus. They were considered devout, learned, proper, and exemplary followers of God. Jesus threatened their systems. These moral religious leaders were betrayed by the weakness of their humanity[32]. Jesus taught, and was the example, of a loving, gentle, kind God. His anger and judgment were reserved for hypocrites, and arrogant religious perfectionists.[33]

When the supernatural Jesus encountered man's religion, the leaders were threatened and sought to destroy Him. They could not rejoice at His message, and accept freedom. They could not recognize God's goodness through their religious pride. At that time, the spiritual and secular authorities were entwined, and they conspired together to destroy Jesus. Many current religious leaders say they are not like the religious authorities that conspired to kill Jesus. Jesus is still knocking on their doors as he did with the churches in Asia Minor.[34].

How can their base leaders dare to speak for God when they have not truly met Him? They are blind to the greatest reality. They do not operate in a significant context and serve a little "g"-god. Despite that limitation, they have acquired great power and masses of followers. I was awed by the magnificent cathedrals of Europe and the power of The Church historically. I then imagined a simple monk named Martin Luther, who was transformed, and challenged such a system. He brought light to millions of people against great religious power with his simple faith.

The highest level of arrogance is to lure the enlightened into a religious structure. It is even more arrogant to try to seize the experience, redefine it, and reduce it to a process or a program. Many people know of God culturally, but have never really met Him. They seek to catch seekers in a false system that diverts them from possible

---

[32] Matthew 23:27

[33] Matthew 12:34

[34] Revelation, 1-4

enlightenment. They work without context for the wrong purposes. They are spiders in a web of deceit. Many dedicate themselves to supporting the system after they have quit seeking God.[35] It is frightening to think of men that stand between God Almighty and His children. When the truth is revealed to them, understanding can break through their deception. That occurred with Saul on his way to Damascus. True brokenness causes them, as Saul did, to leave the system for the wilderness and God.

Looking closer at Jesus, and then His church, I was dismayed at the separation between the two. Jesus spoke to people in the streets, at parties, on hillsides. Now, people lecture about Him in magnificent buildings, with dramatic, logical sermons, soaring music. Jesus spoke truth to convict people in simple places, often individually, to reveal their brokenness and bring them to wellness. Yet, houses of worship entertain, inspire and live in an alternative reality. There isn't a significant difference between the common culture and religions. I realized each person chooses a path to follow and most often, it is the comfortable path that does not reflect the life of God. Being well was too challenging for many people. I still wanted wellness.

The religious masses worshiped gods of their own making, gods which started with a lower case "g". I had seen the stern god, the carnival god, the psychoanalytical god, the god of order and duty. The gods they had created did not reflect the vastness and complexity of the universe, and were petty and tyrannical. I wanted to know the real God; whose name started with capital G.

I considered rejecting theism and seeking answers in the world without God. I found darkness.

---

[35] Matthew 23:15

The Darkness.

Religions are often filled with undercurrents of paranoia, hate, and anger. In Christianity, "The End Times" fed that darkness. Jesus had predicted the Apocalypse for Judea in His generation, and it occurred in the Siege of Jerusalem in 70 AD. That prediction was updated in the late 19th century by John Darby. Believers in modern millennialism now loathe a society that is believed to be their future persecutors.

In their view, society will become a system hostile to believers and will persecute them in a world that God ultimately destroys. The end of the World is now part of the foundation of most evangelical churches. I had lived with that fear and loathing for decades and realized it was unwell. It came from dark hearts and dark minds. I would now become ill when I heard such things.

I met believers that were infected with darkness, their light distorted by it. The World was filled with demons and people conspiring to take over the World and destroy them. The hidden forces in the World were manipulating leaders into acts against God's elect. They were the Rothschilds, the Bilderbergers, the Club of Rome, Davos and the European Union. A universal conspiracy them would take over the world and persecute them. In 2021, many believers have now adopted an anti-science agenda, filled with dark conspiracies by scientists and doctors. The statements they make were paranoid and delusional.

Hurtful events were blamed on spiritual forces which provoked men to evil behavior. I sat through messages that assumed a world filled with evil. They would make statements such as, "the devil made me do it" or "tempted by the devil" or "binding Satan". These beliefs escaped personal responsibility for evil intent within each person.[36] It avoided addressing man's primal nature. I stopped listening to the soul-destroying illness.

The Apocalypse has fascinated humanity for thousands of years. Religious leaders have used that fascination and fear to terrify people into submission. The drama was enjoyed by bored people who enjoy excitement. Even the secular world was filled with stories of the World's end by various natural forces. Such a worldview leads to the emotional sickness that I had lived in for decades. I was heartened when I read that Martin Luther would plant an apple tree if he knew that tomorrow was the end of the World. Breaking free from the Apocalypse released me from the darkness.

Millennialist's come to disrespect society and nature because God will cause ecological destruction and the destruction of man and his society. The belief disengages believers from a doomed reality. It discourages believers from being engaged, from building, and from working for long-term effect. This was illness. We were asked

---

[36] James 1:13

to steward the physical world, which includes nature and mankind, and that we should be active agents of God in our existence.[37] I concluded that the escapism of Apocalypticism was unwell, and that I should be engaged in building and healing as a continuing, investing process.

The Apocalypse came many times for many people. The Apocalypse came for the Jews with the Babylonian exile and then by the Romans in 70 AD. Later, Genghis Khan killed about eleven percent of the World's population in his lifetime. Atilla the Hun killed forty million people in central Europe and Asia. Tamerlane's invasion of India killed about five percent of the World's population. About ninety percent of the natives of North America died during the European settlement. Seventy-Five million people died around the World during World War 2. Most recently, smaller holocausts have occurred in Cambodia, Bosnia, Rwanda, and in Xinjiang Province. For thousands of years, kingdoms have warred in China, India, Europe, the Americas, and the Middle East. These Apocalypses were not mindless slaughter, but were committed by men operating with a belief in their superiority. It shows that man has mastered his physical realm, and now seeks to rule others through struggle and conquest.

Man's soul lives as a bloodied survivor of billions of years of struggle. Modern societies continue to raise totalitarian gods that drive their cultures to dominate others. The next Apocalypse will be triggered by the Dragon, the Bear, or the Djinn. Man is always on the edge of another Apocalypse.

---

[37] John 17:15

Readers may have noticed I did not discuss the Tower of Babel. It is an abstract story from thousands of years ago that had little meaning when I first read it. In the five thousand years since the story was written, man has built many empires that have crumbled through his quest for power. The Tower of Babel was a prediction that man would strive for greatness, but ultimately, his empires would fall. The empires founded on man's wisdom, greed, pride, and power eventually decay internally from man's inner darkness. Now, men are building business empires with malignancies that eat away at the monumental enterprises.

That lust for power was also predicted by the Bible in the stories of Cain and Abel and the fall of Lucifer.[38] It has occurred throughout history in both a great and small actions. I saw men try to dominate others in business, office politics, small town politics, religious organizations, social organizations, families, marriages, and relationships. Even man's latest invention, the internet, is filled with porn, anger, spam, phishing, flaming, and doxxing. When people read the story of Babel, it seems like an abstract story set long ago in the Middle East, but the story predicted humanity's actions for the ensuing millennia. The need for man to control and dominate is innate.

---

[38]Isaiah 14:13-14

In school, my literature courses were filled with darkness. The darkness wasn't new; it could be seen in Shakespeare's works in the 16th century. In *Hamlet*, *Macbeth*, and *Romeo, and Juliet*, people are destroyed by their greed and ambition, leaving only numb survivors. I was drawn to the last words of *Romeo, and Juliet*, "all are punish'd", and *Macbeth*, "[Life} ...is a tale / Told by an idiot, full of sound, and fury / Signifying nothing." In school, I read modern works by Huxley, Orwell, Golding, Salinger, and others, who wrote of man's existence in darkness. Movies, such as films noire, were filled with anti-heroes and horror. I was amazed by people's fascination with those movies. As a student, I treated the arts and literature as entertainment, but now I saw them as expressions of man's darkness, a darkness present in societies throughout history.

I re-read the book of Ecclesiastes to read the thoughts of a successful, brilliant man at the end of his life. When I read it in my youth, it was another abstract perspective. In my later reading, I saw that Solomon concluded his discourse in bitterness, after a life of success. After each success in his life, he concludes that his success was meaningless in the context of eternity. He repeatedly concludes that man should *simply* enjoy the life that we have been given as a gift from God. Solomon was a cynic, and Ecclesiastes is the work of a man that *knew about* God but had not *experienced* God personally. Now, at the end of my life, I understand his viewpoint.

As an alternative to religion, I studied the modern religions of psychology and philosophy. Modern thought sought to understand the unique nature of man, and moved from theology to philosophy, and then to psychology. Existentialism became the basis for much of the studies. It stated that each man should find their meaning independently, apart from social structures and reason. Existentialists admitted that the search led to anxiety, absurdity, and despair. Absolutes and truths were discarded, and reality was based only on each individual's perception. It can be summarized as "It's cool, do your own thing". It was fed by scientific discoveries that undermine man's understanding of time, space and matter.

Existentialism started in the mid-nineteenth century with Soren Kierkegaard and was led by French philosophers in the mid-twentieth century. Sorenson was a godly man that encouraged individuals to seek personal meaning in God. After one hundred years of thought, Existentialism was summarized by Albert Camus, "There is but one truly serious philosophical problem, and that is suicide." Existentialism grew to permeate society and manifested in modern culture in psychology and the arts.

At the turn of the 19th century, William James was born to a family of intellectuals, and became a professor at Harvard. He published his lectures on philosophy, religion, and the emerging science of psychology. James is significant because he reflected and influenced modern intellectual perceptions, which led to psychology. He debunked the pious Pascal and Descartes, both of whom had expounded on living beliefs in God two-hundred and fifty years earlier. Then he acknowledges the rising religious skepticism by intellectuals and agrees with them that there is no proof of God's existence. However, he reasons that it is suitable for man to respond to his religious instincts, simply because the instincts exist. He could not bring himself to use the word "soul", but instead uses Pascal's word "heart". He reflects no personal experience with The Almighty and instead synthesized God as a cold, distant construct. He was the start of modern thought at the beginning of the 20th century.

Psychology emerged as academics studied the soul of man in the mid-20th century. Viennese psychologists moved man's reason for existence from Freud's pursuit of sex, to Adler's pursuit of social power and finally to Frankl's pursuit of meaning. Frankl's essential work is *Man's Search for Meaning*, which documents his 5-year survival in Nazi concentration camps. His associates passed the war in safety, analyzing the neurotic and self-absorbed. In the camps, Frankl saw men stripped to mere existence. He observed that only people that had long-term hope survived. If a person lost that meaning, they died. His experience formed his school of psychiatry, logotherapy, which encouraged men to find meaning.

Frankl carried his lifework into the camp, where it was confiscated and lost. When he received used clothing, he found a copy of the Shema[39], the daily prayer of Judaism, in a pocket of his coat. A spiritually enlightened individual might have taken that as a sign from God. He notes the incident but finds his hope in the idea of seeing his wife again. Actually, his wife had been killed a few months after their arrest, so his hope was in something nonexistent. Frankl remarried after the war, and recreated his life work as *The Unconscious God*. His subtle conclusion is that man needs purpose and meaning, but it does not have to be true or real. His purpose for man was to simply survive with sanity. He encourages belief in purpose to distract men from the "why" of his soul. I could not accept pretending to have a distracting purpose that did not include truth.

Man's search for meaning went from philosophy, to psychiatry, and finally to chemistry. Behavioralists, such as B. F. Skinner, ultimately reduced man to a chemical robot that was programmed by learning and experience. Skinner's path to wellness was by reprogramming the reflexes of the robot. Noam Chomsky then overturned Skinner's theory at MIT. Chomsky recognized the uniqueness of man, which was demonstrated by speech. His example was that an ape (or any other creature), and a human child could receive the same language training. In the end, there would still be a vast difference in speech and thought in the human. He believed the difference was in the deep genetic programming in man that made the difference. Chomsky spent his career seeking to find man's embedded "code" without success. When intellectuals looked at man as a machine, they could not find the soul.

At the same time, Maslow sought to understand man's quest for meaning. Maslow studied healthy human beings to understand man's growth to wellness. He created a tower of needs for man, starting from survival to an ultimate goal, self-actualization. Maslow found the highest level, was not enough. He sensed there was something within man that was above his tower. At the end of his life, he

---

[39] Deuteronomy 6:4

began studying mystical, ecstatic, and spiritual experiences to find something higher than his tower. He observed that the supernatural experiences led to better and healthier behavior. His studies could have led him to God, but Maslow could only be an observer, not a participant.

These men strove to define the uniqueness of man apart from God, and ended up at dead ends. There seemed to be as many schools of philosophy and psychiatry as there were religious sects. The theologians, philosophers and psychiatrists argued, split, and created many different theories. They were a babbling of many clashing tongues. Their works built intellectual Towers of Babel that failed to find the purpose and meaning of man. They tried to create meaning without knowing or acknowledging The Almighty. Their denial of God blinded their theories to man's nature and his primal goal, knowing The Creator. At the same time, simple people understood and experienced that connection daily. Lowly people cleaning their offices had found the meaning of life that the elite sought with decades of thinking, discussion, papers, and conferences. What irony!

Musicians, poets, and writers do not have intellectual pride. They do not need to understand and define existence logically. Instead, they emotionally express what they sense in their souls. Many modern artists create music that expresses an emptiness of existence. My earliest recollections of existential angst in music were The Monkees' *Pleasant Valley Sunday*, The Beatles' *Eleanor Rigby*, and Simon and Garfunkel's *The Sounds of Silence*. Recent music became darker, with dirges like Tears for Fears *Mad World*, Trent Reznor's *Hurt*, or Staind's *Outside*. A significant portion of contemporary music reflects emptiness and separation. These musicians found that ordinary life and its activities were meaningless. Their fame, money, and drugs could not create meaning. Their music reflects a conclusion that man has false dignity and no valid purpose. Their cries of existential angst are heart-rending and echo within many listeners living "ordinary" lives.

This descent into meaninglessness and darkness expressed itself in art.[40] Pictures and photographs became banal or meaningless abstracts. Modern cultures now embrace the antihero as much as heroes. The old heroes are reviled for their weaknesses, not praised for their greatness. It is a cultural revolution that tears down all aspects of society. I had visited some of the great art museums and had seen older, expressive works of art such as Michelangelo's *David* and *The Pieta*, and Rodin's *Thinker*. Now, I walked past jumbles of metal with no discernable meaning that was supposed to be art. Instead of the *Mona Lisa* or the *Sistine Chapel*, I saw drawings of ordinary objects, or meaningless collages of colors. Today's culture screams "meaningless" to the inhabitants.[41]

Philosophy and psychology are the new religions and equally in the darkness as the old religions. Philosophy went from simple existence in Ecclesiastes through to the existentialists. First, "man is a molecule", then "man is a billion tosses of a coin", and then "man is a chemical robot". Reason killed God first, then philosophy, then psychology. Only the hard science of biochemistry was left standing. The modern priests of darkness dwell in academic institutions and lead worship of reason and science. The new demigods are not Bacchus, Ares, and Athena, but are pleasure, wealth, power, reason, the collective, the environment, the Earth.

---

[40] Rookmaaker, *Art and the Death of Culture*

[41] Schaeffer, *How should we then live?*

People seeking answers to the question "why" went to doctors for their emotional stress. The distractions of existence were not enough to stop their pain. Alcohol and drugs could not give them purpose. They sought to find their purpose in existence, but were overwhelmed by messages of meaninglessness in an infinite, unfeeling universe. The medical community treated them with chemistries to lobotomize them, and stop the spiritual pain. The healer's solution to soul sickness was molecules or they urged seekers to find benign distractions to distract them from the search for "why" in their souls. I found this type of medicine as ugly as anything I had encountered in religion.[42] True healing for their souls could be found if they meet God.

In the 19th century, philosophers heralded the arrival of a New Man. The New Men would form a perfect society, unified by the love of a universal community. The New Man had antecedents in the French Revolution and socialist uprisings in the previous century. It continued with Karl Marx in the 19th century and moved to the Age of Aquarius in the 20th century. After hundreds of millions of years of struggle for survival, humanity would suddenly change and find unity and peace. Humanity, united, would dedicate itself to the greater good. Man reasoned himself into an empty servitude to The Collective. The leaders of the New Men slaughtered tens of millions of people in the 20th century. It was a powerfully seductive Babel that men continue to build.

Regressives demonized immunotherapy, food chemistry, genetic engineering, and energy generation to escape the modern World's complexity. They believe regressing to pre-technology will eliminate the pain of contemporary society. The Mother Earth they seek to embrace is filled with predators, harsh climates, and pathogens. The technology they demonized has lifted men from, as Thomas Hobbes stated, a "solitary, poor, nasty, brutish, and short" existence. Men have tried to retreat from progress many times across many cultures. Examples include the fall of the Roman Empire and

---

[42] Ganz, *Psychobabble*c

the Japanese and Chinese introversions over the last thousand years. These escapes fail because change and advancement are unstoppable forces on the planet. Change has been continuous over billions of years. Change will find everyone eventually.

Pastoralists try to escape the burden of existence by becoming one with nature. Women's romance novels tell tales of women finding redemption in a simple, rural lifestyle. The green movement demonizes progress and finds man's end in loving Terra, and living on the land. Even now, some seek to become aborigines in the Information Age. They seek a return to an Eden or Nirvana, and withdraw from society to try to create utopian subcultures. Both secular and religious communities have tried to return to The Garden, believing that regression to Mother Earth would create a paradise that delivers them from modern life. In practice, all these communities have failed because of the sickness within man. Both the Babel and Flood stories predicted the failures to recreate Eden. Over time, man's weaknesses revealed themselves and destroyed Paradise.

Some men are intimidated by the sterility of modern life and revert to aboriginal and barbaric lifestyles. They embrace ancient natural religions. They renew paganism and Earth worship. They worship violence, strength, and conquest. Sports events are organized with increasing violence. Overcome by the complexity of modern life, they seek to return to a barbaric origin and its violence and struggle. Then they go to work the next day.

Man has achieved a God-like level of knowledge of the universe. He understands the atomic, molecular, biological, genetic, ecological, and cosmological structures of existence. Man has manipulated knowledge to create magnificent civilizations. The actions were done by moral free-agents who ultimately worshiped themselves, their people, and their leaders. The result is madness and sickness of the spirit because this knowledge is contained in flawed biochemical shells. The forces inside man have led to cruel actions that leverage his ability to create and exalt in terror and pain. His ancient religious systems did not contain that drive, and when updated to cleaner, rational, modern embodiments, still carry the sickness.

While the carnage of mankind was happening, religions disengaged and became antiquated escapes. It's now entertainment, a place to escape reality or a social life raft. Religious escapism is practiced by men around the World. Religions are now filled with odd theories of the afterlife that have no relevance to the current reality. These religions isolate men from reality. Meanwhile, a secular society has moved into the future, carrying the stain of darkness. Men's religions offer escapism, not healing and truth that confronts and heals people. It's frightening that God says He will remove the light from such a society, if the people given light lose their way.[43]

We live in God's petri dish, and it has infinite walls for us. He has put part of Himself into mankind, which has given us vision to see beyond our confines. Physicist and novelists can see and imagine life outside the walls, but we will not escape our container. We have started to find the limits on our vast, complex world. We have reached the geographical boundaries of the planet, and reached the limits on the definition of the material world. We have described and tamed the biological world down to the microscopic biomes, biochemistry, and genes. Recently, humanity has found the true depths and age of the universe, and found that it is inhospitable and unreachable. The few thousand years of humanity's existence is a thin sliver of time, and the story is playing out. It will be interesting to see what happens in the real end game, at the end of the experiment.

What is the purpose of our souls? The religions across the ages and continents provides evidence that the soul is eternal, and exists in an afterlife. Mankind unconsciously knows that the soul is eternal. We sense an eternal separation from our Creator if we remain without a connection to God. Jesus referred to the separation

---

[43] Revelations 2:5

as "Outer Darkness".[44] The devils with pitchfork and fiery flames were borrowed from Greco-Roman Hades, but the eternal separation and torment will be real. As best I understand it, man's soul would exist in a state of non-existence. Because of this, each person should reconcile with God before death. The possibility of eternal separation is motivation for finding spiritual wellness.

When confronted with eternal separation, many people accept outer darkness as their fate and purpose to enjoy their immediate existence. The irony is that those that believe there is no afterlife will have what they believe, non-life after death. After an encounter with God, people don't worry about the afterlife because they understand an eternal connection to God. I choose to live in that wellness, and not live for the afterlife. My existence is defined by the sermon on the mount, which urges man to live in the presence of God daily.

The early stories in Genesis predicted this result. Man, without God, created demi-gods to rule over us. Historically, I found that man is not healthy as an independent moral agent. He was made from the imperfect physical world. He needs to know God to be truly well. Wellness begins when God is present and fills man's life. I had learned there is a better way in the darkness. How do you live in it?

---

[44] Matthew 22:13

Transformation.

I found people quietly filled with light within churches, typically standing apart from the organization. There was truth behind their peaceful faces. I found the simplest of believers seemed to be the most tuned into God. They lived in religious traditions, but had a deep spiritual life beyond the systems. There was a presence in them that reflected the eternal.

     I was inspired by a woman, M_____, who had met God, and remained in her church. She was short, plump, homely, a little gruff and had a high school education. She was a clerical worker and raised her children. She never held spiritual office, nor was she given a holy title. She met God, shared her spiritual life with others, and inspired them to seek God. She had large gatherings in her home for hours of passionate worship. After worship, she talked about ministering to individuals during her daily activities. She did not teach principles, doctrines, or concepts. Hundreds of individuals were inspired by her, yet she lived a simple life. The spiritual elite never noticed her. M_____ appeared in my life when I was struggling because I knew a lot of theology, but was not living it. She showed me how to interact with God continuously.

Several years later, I saw her obituary in the paper, and decided to go to her remembrance. I learned that she had Alzheimer's, and had spent her last years in a nursing home. Her granddaughter got up and related a story about M_____ at the end of her life. She was lying in bed, with no apparent consciousness. Her granddaughter brought in a tape recorder and played her favorite worship song. As the music played, she raised her hands in worship. M_____ was still teaching people after her death.

I had several companions that had seen God. W_____ was a man that had been seeking God after being born again. I had taken him to a Pentecostal outpouring, and he experienced nothing. We stayed a night in a hotel room as we traveled back from the meeting. As he slept, he saw God as a roaring fire beyond description. He described the experience as being consumed by fire. Another companion, J___ had been born again. He attended a healing rite in a church and was stunned by the greatness of God. The next day, his coworkers noted that his facial expression had changed from anger to peace.

When a person faces The Almighty, it is paralyzing. Man is insignificant in His presence. There is no reasoning or discussion, only awe at experiencing the magnitude of The Creator. It's not filled with humanity or nature; it is infinite and beyond human reasoning. There is no emotion other than awe; there are no human touches. People that have experienced God are marked by infinity. It's rarely discussed because the experience is deep and personal. It is not transferable, nor can it be generated by a formula. They are experiences that occur in unexpected, simple encounters.

Afterwards, life takes on a different context that minimizes the importance of intelligence, feelings, and Earthly struggle. There is an assurance that a powerful force exists far beyond human experience, and it engages with us. Formal religions hint at these encounters, but they are treated as abstract phenomena. Instead, religions substitute complex processes and shallow experiences for an encounter with Almighty God. Minimizing those encounters creates weak, confused people that wallow in spiritual illness.

The Bible has many descriptions of people experiencing God. The book of Job is one of the earliest descriptions about God appearing to man. After leading a pious life, Job is stripped of all his earthly possessions and health. He is counseled by three learned men that lecture about God's character and the cause of Job's suffering. Their discussion and theorizing fail, and God appears to Job. God does not reason with Job, but simply declares His greatness as the architect of existence. The punchline is that there is no convenient explanation, no doctrinal positions, no understanding for Job's fate. The conclusion is that God is God, and He orders the Universe.

God is revealed when a man is stripped of all pretensions and meets God. Job's response was to worship the Almighty. The story of Job is not understood by people filled with reason and agenda, because it doesn't have a reasoned, happy conclusion. It is understood by those stripped of comfortable reasoning and who are reduced to facing the real God. It cannot be taught by learned theologians because there is no satisfying conclusion to the story.

A genuine encounter with God transforms men. They receive an understanding that is beyond reason and beyond feeling. The illuminated have a sense of wonder, and experience a life beyond the natural. The values and knowledge of man are insignificant. These encounters are not familiar to man, and redirect those that have had them with a perspective of infinity. The Bible *does* promise that if a man seeks God truly and deeply, he can meet God. Meeting God brings the ultimate wellness.

Finding spiritual wellness.

"You can't understand light
until you experience darkness" ~MO

So how do you live out spiritual wellness? I had encountered God early in my journey and then gotten sidetracked into religion. Now, I had come full circle, back to the Great God. The time spent lost and confused in religion revealed what was not well, and then led me to find what *was* well. When I got to the point where man's reasoning and religions ended, I met God again. I couldn't understand the light until I had experienced darkness.

Our spirits seek God, but we are bound in a physical body, with passions and struggles in a challenging physical world. Our failures and strivings drain us, but can lead us to seek something more significant. Sometimes it leads to lengthy, complex journeys for spiritual healing. Instead of that labor, we can receive spiritual healing immediately, bringing peace to our souls. That light overcomes our weaknesses as we walk in a dark World.

God *does* meet us in our broken state, and desires to commune with us. It takes faith to initially accept God's grace and then greater faith to continue in that freedom.[45] There is a tendency to want to repay God's love, but it is something foolish in the light of our insignificance. God doesn't need our help. But I saw energetic people working hard to provide God with gifts that have no meaning. This activity often impresses others, and encourages them to do the same. It is a fool's errand. Walking in grace is done daily in humility, in light of our failures, and forgiving other's errors in turn.[46]

Man connects with God by following Jesus' example and teaching. Jesus' death was an example of man's nature meeting Almighty God. Jesus was kind, a healer of bodies and souls. He threatened organized religion, and the religious and secular leaders sentenced Him to death. Jesus demonstrated God's love for man by asking God to forgive his killers. He demonstrated the love and acceptance that God has for mankind.

The life that Jesus taught and demonstrated is the basis for spiritual life. It is different from humanity's religions and secular strivings. Jesus taught us to live a simple life, free from materialism, and instead be filled with the presence of a loving Creator. He taught that we should live humbly, not in arrogance. He taught that we live in a World with error and should forgive errors, as we receive God's acceptance. That forgiveness extends not just to others but also to ourselves. The guilt that is in man makes self-forgiveness difficult. Real self-forgiveness comes from God. Jesus taught that we should be God's children, with an innocent and simple life free from greed and dominance.

---

[45] John 8:36

[46] Matthew 6:12

The best metaphor for being spiritually alive is a lit candle. Historically, candles have symbolized God's presence in Western art. A candle is wax with an internal wick. When a point of intense heat is brought near an exposed wick, the heat evaporates the wax. The gas from the wax is drawn through the wick, and becomes a self-sustaining point of light. The light is sustained by the infinite, invisible air that surrounds it.

Metaphorically, the wax is man's life, and the wick is man's spirit. God is air, which provides the spiritual oxidizer that converts the wax of man's existence into a spiritual life. The candle's flame is a hot gas, a different state and temperature than the candle. Unlit, the candle and man live in the afterglow of God's Creation. If a man's spirit is not raised above the wax of existence, the wick cannot be lit. If the lit candle is covered and cut off from the air, the flame dies, ending spiritual life. When our spirit is made alive, our wax combined with God's oxygen, creates light in our life. Man's spirit is made alive after it is lit.

The front cover picture is a painting by Gerrit Dou from the 1650s called *Astronomer by Candlelight*. Dou lived during the Age of Reason, which was part of the Scientific Revolution. The astronomer has products of the Scientific Revolution on his desk: a spherical globe, a chemical flask, and a book. An ancient idol stares out of the darkness onto the scene. Printed books were a recent invention of Gutenberg, and recorded man's burgeoning knowledge. The spherical globe harkens to Magellan's circumnavigation of the Earth and the recent astronomic discoveries by Copernicus and Galileo. Newly discovered lenses made possible the astronomer's telescope and the recently invented microscope. Telescopes increased man's understanding of the greater universe, and microscopes gave understanding of the microscopic world. The astronomer carefully positions a candle with his hand, representing the Spirit of God within him. The candle provides light to read and understand emerging science.

Dou is making a statement about faith and reason. The astronomer is mankind; the observer: it's us. We consider the nature of reality in the light of modern science, using the light of God. Dou also created many paintings of hermits meditating on The Bible, surrounded by religious icons. The astronomer and the hermit are Dou himself, seeking Truth in God's presence in both science and religion.

I saw a man's spiritual life as a point of light. The area around the light is often filled with great idols. The idols twist the light into grotesque images or block the light completely. The idols can be fear, control, anger, hate, lust, arrogance, or pretension. Some idols were placed by others, and some were built by personal choice. These idols come from selfish lust for power and pleasure. The image I saw is representative of men.

Over time, I began to see that man is destined to walk broken, even if he has been illuminated. Idols remain after people have been ignited because the idols define who they are. They fear removing the idols because they will become something unknown, although they would emit a purer light. They prefer the twisted, dim images, as if they were their true character. Even the most enlightened were never pure. At the end of our journey, when we are freed of our "clay", we will be free to burn bright and clear. In the darkness, we need to forgive others, forgive ourselves, and some need to forgive God.

Some people that I met were angry at God. They were angry about the way they were formed physically, mentally, and emotionally. They were angry about the abuse and suffering they had experienced or seen. They were mad at God for the nature of their existence. To be well, they needed to reconcile with God, who they saw as the author of a pain-filled creation. Such healing occurs by seeking God in the brokenness, and receiving His healing. That process is beautifully shown in the book of Job.

"You can't take others where you have not been." ~MO

There are many false substitutes to knowing and walking in the light. Spiritual leaders offer structured societies, built on man's devising, that have little spiritual basis. They appeal to our hunger for community, structure, certainty, and entertainment. Many of the enlightened exchanged the light of God for these substitutes. They did not want to move above their "clay" nature. They settle for just enough spirituality to provide comfort. The do not want challenges to their idols. The providers of comfort and structure cannot take seekers where they have not been. They have *not* experienced God, are bankrupt. They feed people an artificial reality that fails under the stress of existence.

Pew Research has surveyed the religious sentiments of the United States.[47] They have identified a significant segment of the population that identify themselves as "Dones" that are "spiritual but not religious". These people had been in organized religions, and had religious sentiment, but had separated themselves from organized religion. I am one of them, and many of my friends are Dones. Many of us still attend church on occasion. We are "strangers in a strange land", a people with no organization or definition. There is a studied distance between us and religions.

The Dones threaten religions, because the Dones have found God is greater than The Church. Organized religion looks at them curiously, wondering how to woo them back into their organizations. The Dones and their cousins, the Nones, enjoy social interaction

---

[47] https://www.pewresearch.org/

within churches, but do not identify with organized religion. The Dones and Nones are categories created by modern pollsters and implies a new phenomenon, but Domes are common in history.

The Dones share a common experience with many historical figures, such as three luminaries of the 17th century Enlightenment: Descartes, Pascal, and Newton. Each man had profound encounters with God early in their lives that distanced them from religion, and fed their search for truth in both science and spirituality. All three lived under the weight of all-powerful churches that threatened dissenters. All three had to walk carefully to avoid persecution and death. Descartes fled to the Netherlands, and Pascal was under continuous suspicion of heresy. Newton needed special dispensation to be a professor at Oxford, because he refused to become a clergyman. All three searched deeply into the structure of physical existence and made profound discoveries, while extolling the presence and virtue of The Almighty, who created the science they discovered.

Seeking and finding God is a solitary process. It involves sweeping away the clutter of man and walking into the unknown. In the Bible, those who met God needed to escape civilization and go into the wilderness. Alone, they encountered God. The experiences directed the remainder of their lives. People came out of the wilderness with fire; their lives went far beyond their cultures and moved them to great things. The times of isolation were how God revealed Himself and lit up men.

Spiritual existence is "being" rather than "doing". We do not "do" Christian; we "be" people energized by God. Our "doing" is weak, but that does not affect our "being". We are people who have destinies to fulfill as children of God. We meet God, and from that relationship comes spiritual life. We respond to creation by treasuring the complexity and beauty of our existence. We respond to the marvels of nature, and man's creations in scientific, technical, and artistic works. We enjoy them because we, the makers, were God-designed and understand the power in creating. Even the souls of the unenlightened respond to The Creation.

"Jesus did not come to make us Christians.

Jesus came to make us fully human."

~ Dr. Hans Rookmaaker:"

I love the quote by Dr. Rookmaaker that Jesus came to make us fully human. The words imply that we were not made for religion, but were set free of mere existence. We delight in The Creation and enjoy the complexity of The World that man continues to discover. We can be free of the sicknesses that drives us; we have the opportunity to be free and open people.

I had come across a variety of statements on living the enlightened life. The book of Ecclesiastes recounts Solomon's pursuit of success in many realms. At the end of the search, he concludes that man's goal is to "Fear God, and keep His commandments: for this is the whole duty of man." The Westminster Shorter Catechism from the 17th century Reformation states, "The end of man is to glorify God, and enjoy him forever." I love the mission statement of the Toronto Airport Christian Fellowship, "To walk in God's love, and to give it away". These statements come from people freed to walk with God.

I found some writers who have written about the journey. John Bunyan's *Pilgrims Progress* discusses his Christian experience as an allegory. Bunyan heard some women sincerely talking about God. He went to their Puritan meeting, was changed, and became a preacher. He was imprisoned for non-conformance to the state church for 12 years. In prison, he wrote *Pilgrim's Progress*, an allegory about the Christian life. A believer, Christian, journeys through life, encountering many spiritual adventures. Christian's end is to meet with God in the heavenly city, and dwell with God.

Along the pilgrim's journey, he encounters religious but misguided people. The writing was amusing and adventurous, and Bunyan's allegory fascinated the general public. The book became widely read and applauded. Today, it's considered a child's story, but Bunyan's observation on the sad state of religion was accurate.

I lived Bunyan's journey, but the characters had changed since the 17th century. Instead of Worldly Wiseman and Formalist, there were Rev. Comfortable, Doctor Positive, Deacon Reason, and Elder Guilt. I had adventures in Vanity Fair, the Slough of Despond, and Doubting Castle. As the traveler did in the book, I had become bogged down in my journey, but I had met wonderful people at the correct times that had encouraged me and redirected my path. I was free again.

How do we live?

So how does a lit person live? I have returned to that first encounter when I first met God in simplicity and purity. After my adventures and discoveries, the World has become a wondrous place without the stress of struggle. I was freed, then bound, and now I am free again. I am free to create, to love, to appreciate this existence. We who have met God are not seekers anymore, we are finders. We exist as children of God, our Father., our Creator.

I have met seekers that travel around the World to find meaning. They learned long rituals and self-denial. They sat for months listening to babble, and empty their minds and emotions to escape reality. Some have spent lifetimes studying religion, but have not found meaning and peace. The good news is that God is everywhere and immediately available to everyone. Extensive effort is *not* needed to meet Him, merely an openness to accept His offer of engagement. Afterward, you start your journey by responding to His leading. An experience with God is powerful enough to solidify belief in God to last a lifetime.

My origin was western, logical, middle-class with values of learning, discipline, and obedience. Later, fundamentalists changed my focus to baptism, reading the Bible, prayer, tithing, and fellowship. As I re-read the words of the God Incarnate, I saw a different set of principles to guide a believer's behavior. The different principles were: compassion, freedom from materialism, humility, forgiveness, and truth.

Jesus summarized our existence by quoting the Old Testament: love God, and love men.[48] It is not a law we obey; it is spiritual life that flows from us. Unfortunately, the word "love" can have many meanings and has been interpreted many ways. Some people interpreted this as naïveté and blindness to reality. I met many people who used the concept to escape reality. The love that Christ exhibited went beyond simply existing. His love confronted arrogance and deceit and revealed inner truth to heal. Now, I prefer the terms "compassion", "engagement", and "truth". Love without truth and action is not healthy; it's merely escaping into warm feelings. Love from a relationship with God is active, pure, and healthy.

Jesus said that life should be free from the worship of the physical world. Materialism arises from our biological need to struggle, compete, and seize. That is not the nature of God, nor is it the nature of the soul we have been given. Our deep, quiet soul was given to us to rejoice and interact with The Creation. Ugliness is man's soul exulting himself in triumphs and strength without acknowledging The Creator. That arrogance insults The Creator who gifted us with the ability to create.

---

[48] Mark 12: 30-31

"Cultivate wonder" ~ MO

As I moved towards wellness, I discovered the principle of "cultivate wonder". Wonder occurs when we see things greater than ourselves. "Cultivating" means seeking the wonder in creation. Another word for wonder could be "worship", but it's a corrupted word that calls up dark buildings, intimidating music, hype, agendas, fear, and groveling. Instead, we can enjoy God-designed life with joy. We rejoice in our infinite variety of personalities, experiences, and expressions. Each human is a rich, vibrant creation.

Everything exists for our enjoyment and appreciation. This is our home and workplace; it is not a dark place that we seek to escape. There is an incomprehensible faith that understands that even the events that are cruel, evil, and damaging have purpose in existence. [49] We can appreciate the great works of man, our music, art, structures that are products of our God-given souls. As God underlies the universe, so our souls underlie our creations. In all of The Creation, only man, who has a soul, can truly appreciate the works of a creator.

I have returned to the place I started, but with greater understanding. I have come home from the religious wars. I do not work on the towers of Babel. Now, I am a simple person, filled with the light and joy of my first encounter with God. True wellness is free, peaceful, and straightforward, childlike[50]. It is not burdened with demands, judgment, and agenda. I have no spiritual ladder to climb. I have hope and trust in the Creator beyond my understanding, and I am comfortable with that state. I can engage fully with the truth and complexity of reality, and have purpose and direction. I write these words to help others move down the road to wellness.

---

[49] Proverbs 16:4, Romans 5:4

[50] Matthew 18:3

I have conclusions for multiple people. A first group is distanced from God and merely existing. It may because of self-absorption, skepticism, or an empty religious experience. Please, know that we have a God-given soul that exists to know God as His children. We are more than animals living for power and pleasure. Our purpose and meaning begins when we meet Him. God is here and can be found in an instant. His complexity and depth will be revealed on your journey. He is found when you release your lusts, hurt, and selfishness and move with Him. You can be changed from a caterpillar into a butterfly with the power of flight and a mission.

To those that work in secular and religious swamps: walk away from it. You cannot lead people to a place you have not been. The tools that masquerade as connecting to God are a trap that breaks people spiritually, and buries them into spiritual death. You need to exile from the religions made by man and find God, who will transform you. Do that before trying to move forward. He will take you to a better place when the sickness has been burned from your life. In the wilderness you will find the river. Enter it, and move with the flow. Do not rebuild with the failed tools as have many of the enlightened. Instead, recognize their toxicity to yourself and others. Please do not touch them ever again. Undo the lies that led you to illness, and then continuously walk in wellness. You have been caterpillars teaching butterflies and caterpillars that they can't fly. You have warned them against taking flight and flying away to a distant, unknown destination. Be aware that winter comes quickly. You need to start your transformation; you need start your journey.

To those that are enlightened, let the light shine[51]. We are brought into a relationship with God for more than an interesting experience. The presence of God in our lives permits extraordinary things to move in our lives, and that presence has purpose. Isolating from the sick and living in darkness is cowardly; bringing healing is

---

[51] Matthew 5:16

the noble calling. Avoid returning to sickness, no matter how appealing it appears. Remove the idols from your life as He leads you. Many have lost their way or are corrupted; let your light become pure. You have been transformed and gifted with flight. Don't be caterpillars that merely live to exist; continue to fly.

The Lord Bless You, and Keep You;
the Lord Make His Face Shine on You
and Be Gracious to You;
the Lord Turn His Face Toward You
and Give You Peace.

Numbers 6:24-26

Selah.

The path to wellness.

1. Seek truth, no matter the cost.

2. Live an open, simple life.

3. Connect with God through grace

4. Cultivate wonder.

5. Resist evil and unwellness.

6. Become well, and bring wellness to others.

Model Wellness

SUGGESTED READING

David Aikman, *Jesus in Beijing; …,*

Michael Behe, *Darwin's Black Box,*

John Bunyan, *Pilgrim's Progress.*

Dinesh D'Souza, *What's so Great about Christianity.*

Richard Ganz, *Psychobabble.*

Blaise Pascal, *Pensees.*

Hans Rookmaaker, *Modern Art and the Death of a Culture.*

Francis Schaeffer, *Escape from Reason.*

Frank Viola & George Barna, *Pagan Christianity;…*

YHWH etal, *The Bible*

www.biologos.com

https://www.barna.com/research/changing-state-of-the-church/

https://www.pewforum.org/religious-landscape-study/

Model Wellness

Martin Ogden…

    … spent decades as a scientist and technology developer which gave him a broad understanding of the sciences, which impacted his faith. He is also a student of history, art, music, literature, philosophy and psychology and has observed their impact on modern faith. His knowledge of those subjects has given him a perspective which applies faith across a broad spectrum of life with spiritual truths.

From Martin:

    I hope that this book encourages you to find God in truth and wellness. I continue to seek God in wellness. I invite you to share your journey with me and others. I've set up some points of contact.

www.facebook.com/Ogdonian
Ogdonian@gmail.com

www.ingramcontent.com/pod-product-compliance
Lightning Source LLC
Chambersburg PA
CBHW070726130626
46553CB00005B/2170